THE
TEN DAY
DRAFT

THE TEN DAY
NOVELIST
BOOK TWO

THE TEN DAY DRAFT

A WRITER'S GUIDE TO FINISHING A NOVEL IN TEN DAYS

LEWIS JORSTAD

THE
NOVEL
SMITHY

———

THE TEN DAY NOVELIST SERIES

The Ten Day Outline
The Ten Day Draft
The Ten Day Edit
The Ten Day Author

———

THE WRITER'S CRAFT SERIES

Write Your Hero
Mastering Character Arcs

———

"My aim is to put down what I see and what I feel in the best and simplest way I can tell it."

CONTENTS

Before you go...

Are you struggling to keep track of your story?

If you're ready to get your ideas organized, download your
FREE copy of my Story Bible Template.

It's the perfect companion to this series, and the perfect tool
for creating a clear, bird's-eye view of your novel!

https://thenovelsmithy.com/story-template/

THE LENGTH OF A SEASON

Stephen King once said that, "The first draft of a book—even a long one—should take no more than three months, the length of a season."

While I wouldn't have agreed with him even a few years ago, now I can't help but see the wisdom in those words.

Very few of us will become the next Tolkien. No matter how much we romanticize the slow, tortured process of creating an epic story, we simply won't spend half our life toiling over our magnum opus—our own personal *Silmarillion*—especially if we haven't written a novel before. Though we may one day reach or even surpass literary idols like Hemingway, Rowling, Lee, or Tolkien, we'll never finish our first book if we don't find the will to write it. After all, becoming an author worth reading requires us to write, and write a lot, as we develop and hone our skills.

Despite this, writing a novel remains one of those undertakings most people view as a once-in-a-lifetime event. For them, writing a novel has to take years or even decades, so they slowly tinker away at their story hoping to one day discover a finished draft in their hands. Over time, their motivation fades and the inspiration they started with fades alongside it. There's no endpoint for them to work towards, no final vision of their story to capture. The dream simply goes on forever until, eventually, it fizzles out.

I personally spent years following this same, doomed path, swearing up and down I would write a novel only to drag the process out indefinitely. In the end I always gave up, no matter how much I tried to make that attempt somehow different. Worst of all, I didn't understand why I couldn't stick with it. I'm a sculptor by craft, and a ceramic sculptor at that, so I'm used to projects taking months or even years to complete. Combine that with being a writer and you would think that, if anyone could handle the endless drag of slowly writing a novel, it would be someone like me.

However, in reality I'm like most people—if I'm going to stick with a project I need to see meaningful progress. With a novel, that means chapters completed and scenes written.

This lack of truly visible progress is the real trap writers fall into, myself included. Without a way to see your hard work paying off it becomes harder and harder to stay invested in the story you hope to create. Staying motivated requires you to see a light at the end of the tunnel, something clear and definite to work towards, and planning to finish your novel "someday" doesn't give you that much needed endpoint.

Common wisdom doesn't help here either. Nearly every writer has heard the often-repeated advice: you'll never be a novelist without sitting your butt in the chair and writing. However, what happens when you do sit down, when your fingers do come to rest on the keyboard or grip your pencil in anticipation? What next? Well, for most people, what comes next is months of uncertain work. They have no map to follow, no common path to tread. Writing a novel is an intensely personal process, but even still—for the beginner, without a guiding hand, this personal process can quickly become an impossible one.

Fortunately, there have been efforts to change this.

Events like National Novel Writing Month and Camp NaNoWriMo challenge participants to write a novel in a single month, while similar projects encourage writers to reach their goal over three or four months. What's so great about these events is that they not only push writers to dedicate themselves to their craft, but also make it easy to see real progress. Writers young and old have written hundreds of novels through these events thanks to the structure they provide.

In fact, this ten day challenge is in many ways a continuation of those types of events—the difference is that this book is a guide, not just a framework.

National Novel Writing Month only asks participants to write a novel in thirty days, 1,667 words per day, day after day. On the other hand, this book tasks you with writing a novel in ten days, but it doesn't stop there. It'll walk you through everything from how to prepare yourself to write a novel to how to set realistic goals, manage your mindset, handle burnout, develop a routine, tell others about your project, and organize your story. It'll help inspire you with ways to keep your story's conflict moving and your characters growing, and guide you as you finally wrap up your first draft on Day Ten.

Of course, this won't be dumped on you all at once. This is a ten day challenge after all, and the hurdles you face on Day Two won't be the same you face on Day Nine!

Thus, this book is divided into ten days, with each day guiding you through the challenges you're most likely to face at that stage of your draft. Alongside these chapters you'll also find short sets of goals, ensuring you always know what you're working towards. Ultimately, the purpose of all of this is to give you the tools you need to keep moving forward, so you'll never feel inclined to abandon the challenge.

Because that's the most important thing: sticking with it.

The real secret to writing a novel—whether in a season, a month, or just ten days—is to do it, through force of will, patience, perseverance, and a bit of careful preparation. It can be done. Many before you have done it and many after you will do it again. The choice you have to make is whether or not you'll be one of them.

The purpose of this book is to ease that transition, to help you along as you prove that you are capable of creating something of this magnitude—that there is time in the day, that your story is worth telling—no matter what is consciously or subconsciously holding you back.

This challenge will be difficult, but by the end I'm confident you'll feel it was worth it—so, let's get started.

YOUR QUESTIONS

How should I use this book?

This book is meant to be a step-by-step guide, so you'll find that each chapter is pretty dense as a result. However, don't let that intimidate you! Each chapter has a similar format, which should make them easy to reference while you're writing.

There are two types of sections you'll find in each chapter: mindset and story tips. Mindset is all about keeping yourself inspired, motivated, and healthy during this challenge, while story tips are exactly as they sound—advice for handling the specific story-related challenges you'll face each day. Alongside these sections, there will also be a list of your daily goals at the end of every chapter. If you ever need a quick reminder of what you're doing that day, those goals are where to look.

Additionally, as was the case with the first book in this series, I encourage you to read each chapter and complete its goals before moving on to the next. This will hopefully prevent you from procrastinating on your first draft by reading this book instead!

How much time will I need to dedicate to this challenge?

This question is hard to answer, because a lot will depend on your personal writing style. Ask yourself: what is your average writing speed? How many words could you realistically write in an hour? Consider that you'll be aiming to write around 5,000 words each day and do the math from there.

Of course, some days will be harder and others easier. Still, this challenge does require a significant time commitment— but I'd argue it's well worth the payoff.

Do I have to complete this challenge in ten consecutive days?

No. Unlike this book's predecessor, *The Ten Day Outline*, there are a variety of ways you could take on this challenge. I'll always encourage you to complete it in ten consecutive days, but here are a few other setups I think could work just as well:

- Ten non-consecutive days spread across two weeks.
- Ten non-consecutive days spread across one month.
- Ten non-consecutive days spread across six weeks.
- Ten consecutive weeks.

At the end of the day, everyone has a different schedule and different commitments to keep up with. While I strongly discourage stretching the challenge past ten weeks, you have to decide what's best for you. From here on out I'll assume you're going the ten consecutive day route, but you can easily adapt whatever I'm saying to your specific setup.

Will this be difficult? Is this even possible!?

Piggybacking off the previous two questions, many people wonder if it's even possible to complete this challenge.

To that I say a resounding, yes!

Not only have I done it while testing this process, but other writers have made similar records while competing in challenges like National Novel Writing Month. You'll have to make writing a priority eventually, regardless of whether you write your first draft in ten days or ten years—and personally, I'd rather work hard for only ten days than have my first draft hanging over my head for months.

Like I said above, you'll need to think about your own lifestyle and schedule, but if you do go the ten-day route, know that it's entirely doable with enough commitment and time.

What if I've already started my first draft?

No problem! You'll just have a head start.

If you're already a significant way through your draft, you may need to skim through a few of the early chapters before finding the right place to start from. A good way to speed up this process is to reference The Complete Ten Day Drafting Process at the back of the book.

What if I'm writing a series?

If you're writing a series, you can still use this book to guide you while you work on each individual draft. However, before you get started, I would encourage you to outline your entire series first—though I would encourage that regardless of whether you were taking on this challenge or not!

Is there anything I need to know before I start?

Throughout this book I'll expect a basic level of familiarity with common storytelling concepts like story structure and character development, along with a few other important bits of writing terminology.

However, if you're not an expert on these topics, that's ok.

I'll do my best to explain basic terms and information where necessary to ensure we're all on the same page. This book won't require a tremendous amount of structure anyways, and you may even notice me using a simplified version of the Three Act Structure. After all, your first draft should be more focused on getting your story on the page, rather than stressing out about the more detailed aspects of the craft—outlining and editing are the best times for that.

However, there may still be concepts you would find useful to understand that I simply don't have the space to cover here. Fortunately, I've created a handful of free resources on story structure and character creation that you can find over on my website:

https://thenovelsmithy.com/

Additionally, I'll also be referencing four popular movies as examples throughout this book. While you don't need to have watched them to understand these examples, they're all excellent in their own right and well worth your time! These are:

- *Star Wars: A New Hope* (1977)
- *Princess Mononoke* (1997)
- *Mulan* (1998)
- *How to Train Your Dragon* (2010)

Will I need anything else before I start this challenge?

As you may know, this is the second book in this series, the first being *The Ten Day Outline*. Despite this, everything you find in this book will be usable regardless of whether or not you've read that first book. The main benefit of reading *The Ten Day Outline* will show in how prepared you are for this challenge going in—once you've gotten started, everything else should be mostly the same.

Of course, I won't be offended if you pause to go read *The Ten Day Outline*. It's a pretty good book, if I do say so myself!

DAY ZERO: HOW TO WRITE A NOVEL

R unners don't run a marathon without plenty of water, just like mountaineers don't climb Everest without food and shelter and painters don't create a masterpiece without first gathering their palette and brushes. Likewise, writers don't write a novel without going in prepared.

For any project of this scope and intensity, you want to set yourself up for success as much as possible. This is especially true when you're trying to complete a challenge with such a tight deadline as this one.

That's why, before you can even begin this challenge, you'll need to consider a few important things. Today we'll be talking about all the issues below, while giving you pointers on how to ready yourself for the days ahead:

- Where will you write?
- When will you write?
- What will your goals be?
- What will your story be about?
- Who will you tell?

- And how will you protect your work?

Yes, a "Day Zero" is slightly cheating—this *is* supposed to be a ten day challenge after all—but nothing as major as writing a novel can be completed successfully without a bit of preparation beforehand.

You'll face a lot over the next ten days, so today will be all about getting yourself in the right place to write and your story in the right place to be written.

Choosing Your Writing Space

First up, you'll need a space to write.

Your environment is a huge factor in both your ability to focus and your aptitude for creativity. Few writers—at least that I've found—wrote their masterpieces surrounded by other people and things demanding their attention. Unless you've proven that you can thrive amid chaos, you'll want to find a writing space with few distractions or with distractions you can effectively tune out.

Many writers work from a home office they've set up for this exact purpose, while others like to visit a nearby library or shared work space. Personally, I write at the kitchen table.

What really matters when picking this space is:

———

Comfort:

Do you have a comfy chair? Somewhere that encourages good posture? Writing is an art form that often neglects the physical body, but keeping yourself comfortable and in good physical shape is just as necessary to writing as it is to painting, photography, or jogging.

You need enough stamina and mental clarity to focus for long periods of time, so make sure your chosen writing space provides an environment conducive to your health and wellbeing.

Supplies:

You'll also need to properly equip your chosen writing space for this challenge, and this is another element that varies from person to person. These days I write everything in a program called Scrivener, including random notes and research. This means I only need my laptop, computer charger, and some headphones to work on my novels, but I'll often keep a notebook around as well.

You may prefer to write with pen and paper exclusively, and that's perfectly ok. Just make sure you've thought about what you need to work efficiently and how you plan to store or transport those tools to your writing space.

Focus:

Learning to limit distractions is a huge part of this challenge. No matter how dedicated you are, you won't write even a thousand words if you're constantly losing focus, not to mention fifty thousand. This is about more than just noise too. Everyone can tolerate different levels of noise, so whether you need noise canceling headphones even in your home office or can comfortably write on the subway depends on what kind of person you are.

More important than blocking out noise is eliminating digital distractions: notifications, emails, texts, phone calls, and the Internet. If you do nothing else to prepare for the days ahead, please find a way to shut off the Internet while you work. The Internet is an amazing thing, but it's also a massive time sink that won't help you during this challenge. Even if you think you'll need it for research, trust me—you won't.

We'll talk more about research later on, but for now, be ruthless in eliminating any distractions from your chosen writing space.

Inspiration:

There are two distinct ways to find inspiration through your writing space: you can either work somewhere beautiful or somewhere so drab that you have nothing to focus on but your own creative mind. In the end, this is another aspect of your writing space you'll need to do some soul-searching on. What type of space boosts your creativity the most?

Another way to create an inspiring environment is to listen to ambient music or movie soundtracks, especially if the tone of the music matches the tone of your story.

Purpose:

Ask yourself: is your chosen space dedicated to writing? Previously I mentioned that I write at my kitchen table— which is quite literally not a "dedicated writing space"—so this is more about mental distinction than anything else. While I eat meals and prepare food here at various points in the day, I mentally designate this space a "writing space" by clearing it of everything other than my laptop, notepad, pen, and water. This way my brain recognizes it's writing time, allowing me to zone in on the task at hand.

If you have a home office you can dedicate to writing for the next ten days, that works great, but not everyone can create this separation so easily. In those instances, it can be helpful to find an unusual location, somewhere you rarely frequent like a local cafe or library, and set up shop there for the duration of this challenge. So long as it meets all the other criteria for a good writing space, this can be a great way to show your brain that it's writing time—not answer email, scroll through your phone, or do the dishes time.

———

Once you've found a writing space that both fits these criteria and that you're happy with, gather up any supplies you'll need and either set them up in your new space or pack them in whatever you'll use to carry them back and forth. Now, you can move on to figuring out when you'll be able to write.

Finding the Time

As stressful as it is to manage a schedule, having clearly defined writing time is another important way you can improve your odds of succeeding in this challenge.

Some writers like to write during the same block of time each day, while others write in small chunks throughout the day. Either way works, and it's ultimately up to you. The only requirement here is that you block out a time when you *will* write, come hell or high water.

Of course, we all have busy lives, and this can seem like an impossible task if your schedule is already full. However, I'd argue that's the beauty of this challenge. Yes, you may have to give something up to make time for writing, but it's only for ten days—not even a full two weeks.

So, sit down and pull out your calendar. Look carefully at your schedule and decide which days you'll write, keeping in mind any major commitments that might delay your progress. If you look at your calendar and realize there's simply no way to fit in enough time to complete your draft, you may need to shift the challenge back to compensate. However, don't let yourself feel tempted to give up all together. Eventually, you'll have to decide to write even at the expense of other things, and now is the time to do so. If at all possible, find time within the current month to complete this challenge.

Once you've decided which ten days you can realistically dedicate to writing, you'll want to mark those days on your calendar, while leaving space for something else we'll add in just a moment.

The reason it's so important for you to write these days down is because it forces you to commit to the challenge ahead. You're far more likely to meet your goals if you treat them like you would a doctor's appointment or class—a commitment you've made and won't break. Still, things will come up over the course of this challenge. You'll get sick, you'll need to stay late at work, or your dog will go frolicking with a skunk and stink up your whole house. This is why you should also account for something called "mercy days."

These mercy days are writing days you keep in reserve, as backups for when life throws something unexpected your way. This way, you won't fall behind on your goals even if you miss a day you had originally planned to write.

In the short term this may seem silly—the point was to dedicate yourself to this challenge no matter what, right? Yes, but let's be realistic. Things happen. That's life. By building in mercy days, you're much less likely to give up on the challenge altogether when you inevitably miss a day or don't quite meet your goals. You can relax knowing you have time to catch up and that all is well.

Of course, you shouldn't use these days lightly.

These mercy days are meant as a last resort, something you save for when you truly need it, not something you use because you didn't quite feel like writing the day before. Try to reserve them, using them only to catch up when life throws you a curve ball.

The only exception to this rule would be if you need a mental health day—after all, taking care of your mind and body is just as important to succeeding in this challenge as sitting down and writing. Creating a novel requires tremendous amounts of mental energy and creativity, so creating time to eat healthy food, rest when needed, get good sleep, take walks, and spend time with other people is always worthwhile.

Long story short, once you've marked your writing days on your calendar, add an extra two mercy days for good measure (and do your best to save them for emergencies).

Setting Goals

Another big part of success is setting the right goals, and that's your next task for today. This challenge is meant to push you in every way, so your goals *will* be difficult—but you still want them to be well-thought-out.

The ultimate goal of this challenge is to write a fifty thousand word first draft, the same as you would for an event like National Novel Writing Month. This way you have a good foundation to build on as you move into polishing and editing your novel. However, it's also possible your story will reach its natural conclusion somewhere closer to the seventy or eighty thousand word mark, depending on what you're writing.

This presents a problem: if you've based all of your goals on word count, you could easily get to Day Ten and still be thousands of words away from actually finishing your draft. Because of this, instead of planning your goals around word count it might make more sense to plan them around scenes.

If you're not already familiar with them, scenes are the building blocks of your story, and form the individual events of your novel. Your characters start with a goal, experience challenges trying to reach that goal, and either succeed or fail. The outcome of each scene then flows into the next, dictating your cast's next goal, which is why scenes are the bricks that build your novel—each one rests on the ones before it.

Importantly, scenes are not chapters, which can actually consist of one or more scenes.

Fortunately, understanding your story's scenes can make setting goals for this challenge much easier. Since the average novel has between thirty and forty scenes, you can estimate how many scenes you'll need to write each day to complete this challenge. Based on these averages, if your goal is to write forty scenes in ten days, then you'll need to write roughly four scenes per day. However, this isn't perfect—again, every novel is different, and you have no way of knowing how many scenes your individual story will have.

That's where outlining comes in.

The Value of an Outline

There's no point in beating around the bush—having a well-built outline is essential for this challenge.

Your outline is an invaluable roadmap of your story, and will make it infinitely easier to write consistently. Even if you're the type of writer who normally prefers coming up with your story as you go, you'll still need to have an outline before beginning this challenge.

Unfortunately, there's no way for me to explain everything about outlining in just this chapter. The first book in this series is all about outlining a novel—aptly named *The Ten Day Outline*—so if you have no idea what an outline is or how to create one, I encourage you to read that book first.

Of course, you're not required to have read that book before moving on to this one, nor do I want to force you to use my personal outlining method. While I will reference aspects of my method throughout this book, there are as many outlining methods out there as there are writers, and all of them have their own pros and cons. You're welcome to use any method you like, whether it's mine, one of your own creation, or one of the other popular methods such as those created by KM Weiland or Libbie Hawker.

Instead, let me explain what your outline will need to cover, regardless of which method you use to create it:

———

Your Story's Plot:

To understand your story, you obviously need to know what will happen in that story. How does your protagonist get involved, what core conflict are they facing, how will they try to handle that conflict, what challenges will they face, and how will the story ultimately resolve itself?

You should also have a basic idea of how these story beats line up within your story's structure. For the purposes of this challenge, we'll be using the Three Act Structure, simply because it's so user friendly.

Your Cast:

Just like with your plot, you want to have a good idea of who populates your story's world.

Who is your protagonist and how will they grow and change throughout your story? What lessons will they learn? Likewise, who is your antagonist and what are they trying to achieve? What about supporting characters?

Your Worldbuilding:

This section of your outline can be as long or as short as you want, and will contain the rules that define your story's world. These might include various technological, magical, or scientific systems that exist, along with cultures, religions, languages, social norms, and locations.

This is where the bulk of any research you do for your novel should live, and it's how you'll keep the events and settings of your story consistent and believable.

Your Core Conflict:

While we mentioned your story's conflict under plot, you'll want to make sure it's written on its own as well. In a sentence or two, clearly define what the conflict of your story is and how it will evolve over the course of your novel.

This is a critical piece of the storytelling puzzle, and not something you want to be uncertain of.

Your Scenes:

Finally, you'll want to make a brief list of the various scenes in your story. Each of these should have a short description of what happens in that scene, what your protagonist's goal is, what challenges they face, and the final outcome. You may also want to include a brief note about how each scene moves your cast closer (or farther) from resolving the core conflict of your story.

———

If you follow an established outlining method, your final outline should cover everything on this list in plenty of detail, with one major exception: your scenes.

Outlining every scene in your story is a somewhat controversial practice among many writers. Not only that, but it's a lot of upfront work. While I personally consider it to be an essential step because of how useful it is when building cohesive stories, not everyone will agree.

I'll always encourage you to go the extra mile and outline your scenes before you write, especially with a challenge like this one. However, you can still set reasonable goals without knowing all of your scenes upfront. In the end, the choice is yours. If you want to know how I make the process of outlining your scenes a more manageable one, then check out *The Ten Day Outline.* Otherwise, you can simply set up your outline with the other elements I mentioned and base your goals on a target word count instead.

Once you have either a list of your story's scenes or a general idea of how long your novel will be, you can create your daily goals using some simple math. All you need to do is count the number of scenes (or target words) in your novel and divide by ten—from there you can see how many scenes you need to write each day, as well as exactly which ones.

> **Note:** In future chapters, you'll find that I list sample scene counts (or alternatively, word counts) to help keep you on track as we go. However, these are just examples, and you should insert whatever goals you've created in their place. If you're above or below these example numbers, don't freak out! Reference your own personal goals and, so long as you're on track with those, you'll be just fine.

Returning to your calendar, write the names or numbers of these scenes on the days you plan to write them. Now you have clear goals in place and know exactly what to expect for each day of this challenge.

Of course, as you look through your outline keep an eye out for any scenes that'll be particularly difficult, such as your story's conclusion—these scenes will naturally be longer and take you more time to write. Because of this, it may be worth writing fewer scenes on days when you plan to tackle these more challenging sections of your story. This way, you won't feel pressured to rush.

To compensate, plan to write an extra scene or two on days when you know you'll either have extra time, or will be working on an easier part of your story.

Some Final Tips to Keep in Mind

———

Keep the Well Full:

Perhaps my biggest tip for making consistent progress during this challenge is one I picked up from Ernest Hemingway: stop writing each day when you're still bursting with ideas for what comes next. This often means pausing your work mid-scene, and that's ok. The goal is to never drain your well of creativity completely, that way you'll know exactly how to continue when you sit back down the next day.

Take Notes:

Another way to keep your creativity active is to take notes on anything that sparks your imagination in everyday life. Whether you overhear an interesting conversation at the grocery store or see a beautiful landscape, jot it down in a notebook or in your phone's notepad so you can use it for inspiration if you ever feel stuck while writing.

Find an Outlet:

No matter how hard you try to stay inspired, there will inevitably be times when you get stuck. In those cases, you'll need an outlet. This could be anything from walking to cleaning, exercising, or even taking a bath, so long as you avoid things that are distracting like watching TV or scrolling through the Internet.

Your goal with this outlet is to help your mind zone out, rest, and recharge while not disrupting your creative state—

essentially, to clear your mind of whatever is blocking it so you can continue your story.

Tell Your Loved Ones:

Over the course of this challenge, you may find you need the support of friends and family to help you along. Of course, that requires you to tell them about the challenge first. As intimidating as that may be, doing so before you begin writing can be a huge help.

Don't get caught up trying to explain what your story will be about—it's far better to just hand them your finished novel when it's all done—and instead focus on explaining what the challenge is and why it's important to you. If they have concerns, remember that they probably mean well. Do your best to comfort them, but don't let any negativity they express deter you from completing this challenge. Having their help and support is nice, but not essential.

Find Your Why:

A big part of dedicating yourself to any creative pursuit is having a purpose.

Why are you doing this? Why is it important to you?

This challenge will be a major undertaking and, while surmountable, you'll need a strong sense of your Why to keep yourself going. Do some soul searching here and decide why this novel matters to you. Once you know your Why, write it down at the top of your calendar where it'll be clearly visible as you tackle your goals each day.

Save Your Work:

Finally, you need a way of protecting all your hard work throughout this challenge, especially if you're typing your draft on a computer. There's no worse feeling than having your computer crash on Day Seven, knowing you've lost thousands of words and a full week of work.

To prevent this, make sure you keep a copy of your draft both on your computer and on an extra storage device like a USB. Back it up at the end of each writing session religiously, so you never have to worry. If you're writing in a notebook, this is less of a concern, but I still encourage you to find a safe place to store your draft when you aren't working to ensure it's never damaged.

———

The Goals of Day Zero

We've finally reached the end of Day Zero!

While this may seem like a lot of work, especially considering the challenge hasn't officially started yet, it was all for a good reason. Whether you write a novel in ten days or ten years, you'll eventually find yourself facing burnout—it's simply a natural part of the creative process—and being prepared for it is more important than trying to avoid it.

Day One may be where the real challenge begins, but that doesn't mean Day Zero wasn't an essential step on your journey. By laying the right groundwork now, you'll be in a much more comfortable place to succeed later.

Tomorrow we'll officially begin this challenge, but for now, here are the goals you've completed for Day Zero:

1. Find a space that nurtures your creativity and set it up with any necessary supplies.
2. Mark ten writing days and two mercy days on your

calendar, keeping in mind any major commitments that might delay your progress.

3. If you don't have one already, create a brief outline that covers your story's plot, characters, worldbuilding, conflict, and (optionally) your scenes.
4. Based on the number of scenes in your outline, set goals for yourself and add them to your calendar.

On to Day One!

2

DAY ONE: FINDING THE RIGHT MINDSET

Aside from physical preparedness—pencils, pens, or even a decent word processor—there's nothing that influences your ability to write a novel more than your mindset.

Mindset is a huge part of writing a novel. This is a massive project you're about to embark on and, as we discussed yesterday, setting yourself up for success is as important as sitting down and writing to begin with.

Since today is the first day you'll be doing some serious writing, we'll be focusing on mindset a lot in this chapter. Later chapters will have much more emphasis on story tips and advice, though you can still expect some discussion of mindset in every chapter. Since the mental hurdles you face on Day One will differ greatly from those you face on Day Nine, there will always be new things to discuss. Still, today will have by far the most focus on mindset of any day in the challenge.

Specifically, today you'll need to embrace the inherent messiness of your first draft. We'll get into more details in just a moment, but suffice it to say that no first draft—not even Stephen King's or J. R. R. Tolkien's—is perfect. Yours won't be either.

Of course, there are a few technical things to cover as well.

Alongside mindset, we'll be setting up the start of your story, tackling your opening line, and introducing your first few characters. There are a lot of firsts to deal with today, but don't worry—we'll ease our way through them all and, by the end, you'll officially be on your way to a finished first draft!

The Real Purpose of the First Draft

As I mentioned earlier in this book, I spent nearly a decade of my life as a ceramic sculptor. Though I've moved away from sculpting in recent years, playing in the mud—while not glamorous—was deeply creatively fulfilling. All jokes aside, when I began shifting more of my focus towards writing, I figured none of the lessons I'd learned as a sculptor would carry over.

I was very wrong.

You see, creating a sculpture and writing a novel follow nearly the exact same process. When creating a new sculpture I would sit down and sketch out a picture of what I wanted to create, before diving in and forming the rough shape. From there, I would add chunks of clay here and cut away pieces there until I had something that vaguely resembled the idea in my head. This was, essentially, my first draft. Only once I had finished this rough figure could I carve the finer details, polishing the whole piece until it was complete.

By the end of this process the finished sculpture might look nothing like my original draft, but that early form was an essential part of creating the final shape. The same will be true for your novel—without a messy first attempt you'll never be able to polish your story into the finished book it'll one day become.

Unfortunately, many, *many* writers stall out in a futile quest to write a perfect first draft. Perhaps you've never felt this way before (lucky you), but I imagine at least a few of you are here precisely because you've fallen into this trap.

While taking on this challenge you need to remember that the first draft's job is only to get your ideas on paper, and that's ok.

Editing is where your story will truly come together, but that's a task for another day. First you need a foundation, and while you'll naturally want to create a strong draft to edit from, there's no point getting caught up trying to write a *perfect* first draft. All that will do is cause you to burn out faster, writer slower, and feel unnecessary stress. By simply relaxing and letting your creativity take hold, you may create some true gems you wouldn't have thought of otherwise.

So, before you write today, embrace the terrible first draft. Remember this mantra: "My first draft doesn't need to be good."

My sculptures weren't any good when I first formed them, and your novel won't be any good at this stage either. Most importantly, it doesn't need to be—perhaps it even shouldn't be. After all, there's no writing sin you can't correct in editing, but never finishing your draft to begin with is unfixable.

The Challenges of Starting a Story

Of course, even with the right mindset the first few scenes of your novel will be challenging. Not only is it hard from a writing perspective—you're introducing a whole new world and cast after all—but it's also hard from a mindset perspective. Your brain simply isn't in the writing zone yet, and it'll often feel like you're fighting your way through quicksand to write another word.

At the end of the day, this early hurdle is unavoidable, but there are ways to help yourself move past it.

For starters, don't let this feeling concern you. As you get deeper into your draft, words will flow more easily and your brain will get used to writing. You'll learn how to tap into your creativity and your overall writing will improve—seriously, in every manuscript I've ever edited I could literally see where the writer finally hit their flow state!

You may also find yourself trying to emulate other authors at this early stage, even if only subconsciously. This is normal for many writers, especially if you haven't discovered a distinct writing voice of your own. You've spent so much time falling in love with other people's stories that you'll naturally want to channel that style in your own writing. Perhaps on some level you feel that mimicking their style might even make your novel just as good as theirs... right?

Unfortunately, that's not how a writer's voice works.

While we do cultivate our writing voices by reading other authors' work, struggling to emulate their style word for word usually does more harm than good. After all, you're trying to tell *your* story, and telling it in your personal voice is the most powerful way to do so. Not only that, but you'll fail to write anything if you're too busy fighting to make it sound like this or that author—it's yet one more thing that'll slow you down and frustrate you at this early stage.

Instead, let go of any desire you may have for your writing to sound a certain way. You can always tweak and polish your prose during editing, but for now simply write however comes most naturally to you. By the time you're ten scenes into your story, you'll have not only laid a solid groundwork for your readers, but you'll be more comfortable with your writing as well. Everything you write will be markedly better as a result.

For now though, don't panic if your story doesn't come easily. Stick with it and, in time, you'll find yourself free and clear on the other side.

A Few Early Decisions

Once your mind is in the right place, you're ready to begin your first draft! However, before you can write the first word, you have a few decisions to make:

- What tense will you tell your story in?
- What point of view will you tell it from?

It's possible you've already decided these things (especially if you followed along with my outlining method from *The Ten Day Outline*), in which case you can skip to the next section. If you're unsure how to answer these questions, then continue reading.

These kinds of questions can often trigger a "deer in headlights" moment for many writers. Tense and point of view are a few of the big decisions made early in a novel's life that influence how you tell every other part of the story. Remember though: your first draft doesn't need to be perfect. If you get halfway through this challenge and decide you hate the point of view you've chosen, you can always switch midway through. For now, it's not worth sweating the details, but it is important to have a general idea of how you'll tell your story in the meantime.

So, first up, let's talk about tense. There are a few types of tense to choose from, depending on the type of story you want to write:

- **Past Tense:** I ran, they walked, it saw, et cetera... This is one of the most common tenses used in fiction, and it's a good option for almost any story. It's versatile and unobtrusive, and most readers are used to seeing stories told in this tense.
- **Present Tense:** I run, they walk, it sees, et cetera... This is another common tense used in novels, especially when the author wants readers to feel the immediacy of a story's action. Present Tense allows everything to unfold in the moment, though that does mean characters can't reflect on things that haven't yet happened in your story, which is possible with Past Tense.
- **Future Tense:** I will run, they will walk, it will see, et cetera... Writers rarely use this tense in fiction, and it's really best for experimental or literary novels. Think carefully about whether or not Future Tense fits your story before choosing this option, as it'll require an expert hand to pull off effectively.

Take a moment to consider the options above, and then write your choice down either in your outline or at the top of your draft.

Of course, it's very likely you'll accidentally shift between tenses as you write your first draft. Again, this your story's tense isn't set in stone. By deciding on your tense now, you're simply giving yourself a rough framework for how you'll begin your story. Tense is one of the big things you'll focus on when editing your first draft, so it should only be a minor concern here.

Once you know what tense you plan to write in, you'll need to decide your story's point of view.

This is a significantly more important decision than tense, because point of view determines who tells your story and how much information they have. For instance, if an outside narrator is telling your story it's possible for them to know every characters' thoughts at once. On the other hand, your protagonist can only know about things they hear or experience, allowing you to create different surprises and twists throughout your story.

All the points of view commonly used in fiction have their place, so let's look at what they are and what types of novels they work best for:

———

First Person POV:

In this point of view, the narrator of your story is also one of the characters, usually the protagonist. They tell the entire story as "I did/thought/felt/saw/etc..." This means the story is limited to what the narrator experiences.

- **Example:** Harper Lee's *To Kill A Mockingbird*

Peripheral First Person POV:

This is the same as regular First Person point of view, except in this case, the narrator is not the protagonist. Instead, they're a secondary character, and the reader is limited to seeing the protagonist's story through that peripheral narrator's experiences.

- **Example:** F. Scott Fitzgerald's *The Great Gatsby*

Limited Third Person POV:

Third Person point of view is where the narrator is not a character within your story at all. Instead, they tell the story as an outside observer, recounting it using he/she/they.

In limited Third Person point of view specifically, the narrator tells the story based on the experiences of a single character, usually the protagonist. They can only guess at what other characters are thinking based on expressions and conversations, much like First Person point of view.

- **Example:** Jack London's *White Fang*

Omniscient Third Person POV:

This point of view uses the same he/she/they pronouns as limited Third Person, but an omniscient narrator has access to every characters' thoughts and feelings, regardless of which character the story focuses on. This means they can discuss everything that's happening to every character within the story simultaneously.

- **Example:** Nathaniel Hawthorne's *The Scarlet Letter*

———

When choosing your novel's point of view, focus on who is best equipped to tell your story. Do you want it to be more personal, like it's being told by a friend? In that case, First Person is a good choice. On the other hand, if you want to create a thriller where your reader knows about clues and developments your characters don't, Third Person would be a better option. Regardless of what you choose, your focus should be on what information the narrator has and, through them, what information your audience has.

With your point of view decided on, write it either in your outline or at the top of your draft alongside your story's tense.

Starting Your Draft—At Last!

Finally we can get into the meat of today's goals, starting with another question: how will your story begin?

There are tons of options here, as many as there are stories, but many of them follow a similar pattern. This is where you'll want to start leaning on your outline, since you'll need to know how your story's main conflict gets started in order to introduce your reader to this new world.

Here are some common ways writers begin their stories:

———

Prologue:

This is an opening scene that happens outside of your main story, often in the distant past or future. It's best used to showcase information or events that are critical for your reader to understand, but that you wouldn't necessarily reveal during the normal course of your story.

For instance, two characters might recount a prophecy that foreshadows your protagonist's journey, setting the stage for their adventure. However, be careful to ensure your prologue truly connects back to your main story, as these can often become extraneous.

En Media Res:

Literally meaning "in the middle of things," en media res opens your story in the heat of the action—whether that be a massive battle, an embittered argument, or a dangerous escape. You'll be skipping over the exposition your opening scenes would normally provide, instead filling it in gradually as your story continues.

The Normal World:

With this opening, you begin your story by showing the everyday life of your protagonist. They wake up, brush their teeth, walk to work, et cetera. This provides a great contrast when your story's main conflict enters the scene, but you need to make sure you're still introducing some form of conflict here. Otherwise, your readers are likely to get bored and walk away.

Dream Sequence:

This opening is similar to a prologue, except it's told from the perspective of your protagonist. The dream sequence is a great way to foreshadow later developments in your story or even to recount a past event that's haunting your protagonist. However, this suffers from many of the same pitfalls as prologues. This opening dream should always relate closely to your story's conflict, or it risks becoming a throwaway.

Framing Device:

If you've ever watched *The Princess Bride* or read *City of Thieves*, you'll be familiar with this opening.

The framing device is essentially a secondary narrative that "frames" your main story, often told by an outside narrator who recounts the events of your novel to the reader or to another character. This is a great way to add extra context and weight to a story, especially one with historical significance, though it's just as useful for comedic affect as well.

———

Regardless of which opening you choose, every novel needs to begin with some kind of conflict. This could be anything from an intense shootout to spilling a morning coffee, so what's important here is how this opening conflict relates back to the main conflict of your story.

In some openings (such as En Media Res) the conflict of this scene will be directly tied to the main conflict of your whole novel. In others, your opening conflict may be something small that simply reveals an important fact about your characters or world. The key here is to think carefully about your reader's first impression of your story. Your opening is a promise to the reader, so meandering alongside your protagonist while they have an uneventful grocery trip won't quite work for a hardcore action trilogy. However, it might work perfectly for a more introspective romance novel, especially if the grocery clerk is a suave love interest!

Alongside deciding how to open your story, you'll also need to craft an opening line. This is another one of those panic moments for many writers, and I can only imagine the hundreds of novels writers have abandoned simply because they couldn't get past the opening line.

Yes, this is something you can agonize over for years.

No, that doesn't mean you should.

In reality, the opening line doesn't matter that much—at least not at this stage. Just like everything else you write throughout this challenge, you'll tweak and perfect your opening line later. Today, your opening line only matters in that it's one more hurdle between you and the start of your draft.

Starting your novel is all about building and maintaining momentum, meaning you shouldn't be spending an hour tinkering with your opening line. Some writers are zen enough to write whatever comes to mind, trusting that they'll edit it down the road. Others might steal a famous line from another novel and then replace it with their own later on. Personally, I like to write gibberish until I hit my stride, often making a list of random bullet points until inspiration strikes. Whatever you have to do to get those first few words on the page, just do it. You'll get to come back and improve upon it later.

Finally and far more importantly than your opening line is what should immediately follow it: your story's Hook.

Remember that conflict we talked about when discussing how to open your story? Well, this is it. The Hook is the first of the six major plot points within the Three Act Structure, and it's meant to grab your reader's attention and get them invested in your story's world. As a result, this should almost always be the first scene of your novel. Fortunately, your story's Hook is one of the simplest plot points you'll have to deal with.

At its core, the Hook introduces your reader to a unique aspect of your story's world or characters and then cements that interest by attaching it to some form of conflict. This conflict can be anything, like we discussed earlier, but it should relate back to another important aspect of your story.

For instance, here are the Hooks of our four example movies:

- *Mulan*: *Mulan*'s opening scene shows the moment the Huns scale the Great Wall of China and begin their invasion. This not only sets up the main conflict of the entire movie, but sets the tone for what's to come.
- *How to Train Your Dragon*: Hiccup's adventure starts en media res when a group of dragons attack his village. This Hook not only introduces the unique concept of a world full of dragons, but also introduces us to Hiccup's struggle to be accepted by the other Vikings. All of this ties directly into the main conflict of the entire movie, that being the fight between the Vikings and the dragons.
- *Princess Mononoke*: Much like *How to Train Your Dragon*, *Princess Mononoke* starts en media res. A demon is attacking Ashitaka's village, and he has to jump in to stop it. This Hook sets up the main conflict of the story, while also introducing the crucial detail that this is a world shaped by demons and nature spirits.
- *Star Wars: A New Hope*: *A New Hope*'s opening could be considered both a prologue or en media res, depending on your interpretation. The Hook follows Darth Vader as he intercepts Princess Leia's ship and

takes her hostage. However, she's able to get the Death Star plans off the ship with R2-D2's help, sparking the conflict of the whole film.

As you can see, each of these Hooks introduces something unique about their story, while also relating back to the main conflict of the film. Of course, your novel will have a bit more time to set up many of these important elements than a film would, so you don't necessarily need your Hook to be as laser focused as these. However, these are still a great example of Hooks used to their fullest potential, with no wasted space.

Overall, conflict is key here. Whatever conflict you choose for your Hook, make sure it encourages your readers to ask, "What will happen next?"

An Important Introduction

Once you move past your Hook and into later scenes, you'll start introducing your story's world and cast to your reader —meaning this is your chance to establish the basic rules, settings, and characters of your story!

Alongside these more general things, you'll also be introducing one specific (and very important) element to your reader: your protagonist.

Whether they're introduced in the very first line of your draft or not until the end of the Hook, your protagonist's introduction is a big moment for your story. This is their chance to make a solid first impression, so you'll want to think carefully about their defining characteristics.

- How do they view the world?

- How do they carry themselves?
- How would you describe them? Welcoming, harsh, inquisitive, anxious, kind…?
- What are their current goals? Desires?
- What flaws do they have, and how do these manifest in their actions?

While it's a tall order to cover all of these traits right away, thinking about them ahead of time can still help you incorporate them in subtle ways.

As a side note, I encourage you to stick closely to your protagonist in these early scenes. Your reader won't feel fully invested in your story quite yet, so you don't want to overload them with subplots and side characters at this point in your novel. Instead, focus on your main conflict and on the experiences of your protagonist. While we won't talk about it for another three days, there will be an entire half of your story dedicated to exploring your cast and the many subplots that may arise from them. Now isn't the time for side content, but don't worry—that time will come!

The Goals of Day One

As we wrap up our first full writing day together, I want to leave you with a few final tips:

———

What if you didn't meet your goals?

Depending on how long it took you to find your groove, it's very likely you didn't hit your goals for today—and that's ok.

You're still getting into the swing of things and it's normal for the first day or two to go slower than later ones, especially since we're covering so much foundational information. While you should always do your best to meet your goals, you should find yourself naturally catching up as we go forward.

How can you make things easier tomorrow?

Perhaps the best way to set yourself up for success is to finish each writing session with a few sentences of tomorrow's scene already written. This way you can pick back up right where you left off, without struggling for ideas.

Additionally, I find it helps to read books in a similar genre to whatever you're working on between writing sessions. This helps keep your mind in a creative zone, while still being a relaxing way to take a break. Plus, you may get some great inspiration for your own story!

Can you edit as you go?

You may feel inclined to edit your writing as you go through this challenge, but here's my warning—don't. Write each scene and then allow yourself only five minutes (as a hard limit) to read back through and correct any glaring issues. Otherwise, you risk distracting yourself and wasting hours or even days fiddling with your draft. If you find anything major you want to fix, simply make a note in red so you can find it again when it comes time to edit.

———

Finally, I want to finish today by saying: congratulations!

With Day One complete, you've made it over some of the biggest hurdles of this challenge. Today was by far one of the longest and most involved chapters in this book, and the material you covered in your draft was no cake walk either. However, you've proven it's possible. Now, all you need to do is keep your streak going as we move on to Day Two!

Tomorrow we'll peer deeper into your protagonist's inner self, but for now, here are the goals you've completed for Day One:

1. Master your mindset and embrace the idea of an imperfect first draft.
2. Choose a tense and point of view for your novel and write them either in your outline or at the top of your draft.
3. Hook your readers with the opening scene of your story.
4. Introduce your protagonist, along with any basic information about your story's world, settings, and characters.

By the end of today, your draft should have approximately four completed scenes (or five thousand words) and your story's Hook should be complete.

On to Day Two!

DAY TWO: DEVELOPING A ROUTINE

W hen you wake up in the morning, what do you do?

If you're like me, you might wash your face, brush your teeth, and get dressed. Perhaps you shower and put on makeup, or maybe you go to the gym after walking your dog. Regardless of what your mornings look like, let me ask you: do you have to think about what you're doing, or has it become automatic?

Ok, I get it—going to the gym might not be a breeze *every* morning, but by and large I imagine your morning routine has become second nature. This is the power of routines, and why creating them is such an effective way to both develop new habits and revitalize old ones. Most of the time we never need to think about our routines—instead, they slot in as a natural part of our lives, the same as sleeping or eating.

This is why having a routine is such an important part of being a successful writer, though what that routine looks like will mean something different to everyone. Some writers habitually work at the same time of day every day, while others write in random spurts whenever inspiration strikes them. Some only write in their favorite chair by the window, while others work in cafes and hotels across the world. Regardless of what your personal routine looks like, creating a reliable one will help you tremendously throughout this challenge.

Of course, that's not all we'll need to cover today.

Within your story, a couple of big things will be brewing. Not only will you start diving deeper into the goals and flaws of your protagonist, but you'll continue to explore your story's world and introduce your readers to everything there is to see and do. Most importantly, you'll begin ramping up your story's conflict as you prepare your protagonist for the first major turning point of their adventure!

Your Inner Editor

When most people hear the term "routine," they think of things like time of day or location. However, like I mentioned above, different writers work in all kinds of environments and on all kinds of schedules. Your physical routine will be personal to you and it's something you'll have to hone in on over time.

This is why, instead of trying to prescribe a set routine for you to follow, today we're going to talk about how you can keep your chosen routine productive no matter what it looks like—and perhaps the most important aspect of this is restraining your inner editor.

Your inner editor is a dangerous creature, one that can not only slow your progress, but stop it entirely. This editor is the nagging voice in the back of your head that tells you your writing "isn't good enough," a strange concoction of self-doubt and perfectionism that has held back many a writer. Not only does it make it harder to begin writing at the start of each session, but it can distract and distress you while you're writing too.

Unfortunately, no matter what you write or how excellent it is, this voice will always be there in some capacity. It's a natural part of being human, and while it can be helpful when you sit down to edit, it can only hold you back here. Fortunately, by developing a consistent routine you can find ways to mute this editor.

The goal here is to cut your inner editor off at its source, refusing to give it any more fuel for its fire. There are a few ways you can do this, so try mixing and matching these to fit your personal writing style and routine:

———

Start Fresh Each Day:

Your inner editor loves to obsess over your previous work, making it easy to waste hours of your time reading what you wrote yesterday.

Instead of allowing this to happen, start each writing session with a blank document or a new page in your notebook. Copy and paste a paragraph or two from your previous writing session to help you remember where you left off and continue working from there. This way, it's far more difficult for your eyes to wander over previous scenes and accidentally trigger your inner editor in the process.

Set Limits:

Just like it's easy to get distracted by your previous writing mid-session, it's also easy to never write at all if you're too busy editing yesterday's work. While it can be nice to edit your draft here and there, you need to set hard limits to keep your inner editor in check.

Personally, I like to set a timer for fifteen minutes at the start of each writing session. Until that timer rings, I can edit to my heart's content, but once time is up I have to begin writing again. Of course, this may not work for you if you write in short bursts, so tweak the time limit to fit your schedule and habits.

Use Index Cards:

This is actually a tip from the first book in this series, *The Ten Day Outline.* Often, you'll need to search through your draft for specific information before you can begin a new writing session. In the process, you'll inevitably get distracted by your inner editor and the cycle of self-doubt will take hold.

Instead of letting that happen, make a point to write down any relevant information for each scene you plan to write on an index card. Whether you do this by brainstorming or referencing your outline, try to avoid flipping back through your draft as much as possible. Now you can quickly reference your index cards as you write, instead of getting sucked down the rabbit hole of your entire first draft.

Take Breaks:

Finally, take breaks throughout your writing sessions. In many ways, this is just as important as not looking back through your draft. All of us have a natural limit where our brain simply shuts down, and if you try to force yourself through this haze you'll end up psyching yourself out. Writing will suddenly feel extremely hard and you might find yourself wondering if you've lost your touch. Here's the secret: you just need a break.

Step away from your story for ten or fifteen minutes and enjoy the outlet you chose back on Day Zero. Whether you take a short walk or wash the dishes, return to your draft and start again. It might surprise you what a difference taking regular breaks can make.

———

Ultimately, your personal writing schedule will be all your own, but by incorporating these into your existing routine you can not only make it more productive, but more enjoyable. After all, listening to your inner editor all day does not a happy writer make!

Sparking Conflict

At the center of any good novel is an equally powerful conflict. Not only will your story's core conflict shape the progress of your plot and the journey of your protagonist, but it'll give your characters something meaningful to pursue throughout their adventure. This core conflict is also what gets your readers invested for the long haul, which is especially important for anyone hoping to publish their novel!

As you might imagine, this means it's critical that you establish the conflict of your story early in your draft. While it's possible that your opening scenes already introduced this conflict—specifically if your story opened en media res—

more often than not the core conflict won't rear its head until a few scenes into your novel, placing it squarely within today's goals.

Thus, a big part of your writing for today will involve either establishing or fleshing out your story's core conflict. Once you've introduced this conflict, you'll also need to push your protagonist to get involved with it—without a protagonist engaging in the conflict, you don't have a story after all!

Fortunately, if you followed along with the goals from Day Zero, you should already have a core conflict in mind.

These conflicts can come in many forms, from galaxy-wide wars to interpersonal battles between two lovers. Often, when we think of conflict we think of physical confrontation, but conflict can be emotional, mental, or spiritual as well.

For example, the core conflict of *Mulan* is the fight between the Hun invaders and the Chinese people. Throughout her journey Mulan, will face a variety of smaller challenges caused by this larger conflict, from minor ones like waking up late for training to direct confrontations with the leader of the Huns. Likewise, the core conflict of *A New Hope* is the Rebel's struggle to destroy the Death Star, and Luke will face a similar variety of challenges born from this conflict.

As you can see, we can sum up both of these movies' conflicts pretty succinctly. However, the creators of these stories didn't sit their audiences down and say, "Ok, so here's the conflict."

Instead, they showed that conflict in action. More specifically, they showed how it interrupted and ultimately changed the lives of their respective protagonists.

Up until now, your protagonist has likely been living their normal life, unaware or unconcerned by the larger conflict brewing around them. However, this can't continue if they're going to leave on any kind of journey. After all, it's far easier to remain in our normal lives than face change or uncertainty! This is why you need to introduce your story's conflict now—not only for your reader but for your protagonist—as this conflict will be the spark that begins their adventure.

Mulan first learns of her story's conflict when the Emperor's messenger arrives in her village. The Chinese army is gathering men to join the war effort and they expect each family to provide one man for the draft—and since Mulan is an only child, her elderly father is the only one who can go. Likewise, Luke hears of his story's conflict when he finds a secret plea for help hidden in a broken droid. His curiosity piqued, he sets out to find out what it means.

As you can see, these conflicts aren't just introduced as peripheral concerns in each characters' life. Instead, we immediately see how these new developments affect the character and prompt them to take action.

In fact, this is the next major puzzle piece you must address for your story: how will your protagonist respond?

Your Protagonist's Motivation

At the end of the day, a story's core conflict is only truly meaningful when it asks the protagonist to take action. By connecting to their personal goals and desires, your story's conflict becomes the catalyst that changes their life. It gives them a reason to begin their adventure and creates the motivation they need to stick with it.

Without this drive your protagonist would have no reason to begin their journey at all, and this is why it's so important to give them compelling motivations that'll last throughout your novel. Not only that, but these motivations need to connect to your story's conflict in some way.

As I'm sure you can tell from the examples above, your protagonist's motivation will largely come down to their core desires. Mulan is seeking validation, and Luke craves adventure. This desire is their want, and this will connect to all of their goals throughout your story. However, in the world of character arcs this want is only half the picture.

Speaking of which, we should start by laying down some quick definitions.

For starters, a characters' arc is the inner journey they go on throughout your story. They start out dissatisfied with their life in some way, and through their adventure they'll be forced to confront whatever flaw is holding them back. After starting their journey they'll face a series of tests and trials, undergo a turning point about halfway through their adventure, and then face a painful setback before finally (hopefully) overcoming their inner struggle and completing their arc.

Choosing which characters have arcs or not could be a book all its own, but suffice it to say that your protagonist is the only character *required* to have an arc of some kind—their arc will be integral to keeping your reader invested in the journey, and will provide most of the emotional payoff we'll discuss later. Your other major characters might also have arcs, but unlike your protagonist this is up to the unique needs of your story.

In total, there are three types of character arcs you might find:

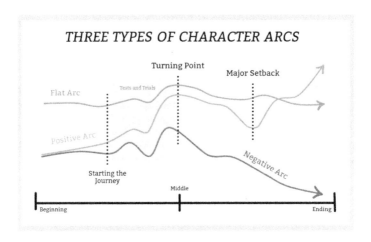

THREE TYPES OF CHARACTER ARCS

Flat Arc

Tests and Trials

Turning Point

Major Setback

Positive Arc

Negative Arc

Starting the Journey

Middle

Beginning

Ending

Positive Arc:

This is the classic "hero" story, though it can apply equally to many types of characters.

In a positive arc, the character starts out with a deep internal flaw. Throughout the course of their arc the story's conflict punishes this flaw. They face a major challenge that leads to a turning point in their arc, moving them closer to uncovering the lesson they need to learn. Ultimately—despite setbacks along the way—they learn to embrace this new truth, overcome their flaws, and succeed against the conflict of their story.

- **Examples:** Rick Blaine, Moana, Aragorn, Han Solo, Hiccup Hiccup Horrendous Haddock III

Negative Arc:

Negative arcs follow a similar trajectory as positive arcs, with a major change at the end.

Just like a positive arc, the character begins the story with an internal flaw and—as the story progresses—uncovers an important truth, experiencing a key turning point along the way. However, unlike a positive arc, a negative arc character rejects that truth repeatedly. By the end of the story they're more entrenched in their flaws than before, growing into a worse version of themselves and failing to resolve the conflict of their story as a result.

- **Examples:** Anakin Skywalker, Jay Gatsby, Michael Corleone, Tyler Durden, Sansa Stark

Flat Arc:

These are the black sheep of character arcs. While positive and negative arcs are "change arcs," a flat arc character already knows their truth (or lesson) at the start of the story. Instead, their arc is about upholding that truth in the face of their story's conflict, passing their lesson to others in the process.

- **Examples:** Captain America, Katniss Everdeen, Luke Skywalker, Princess Nausicaä, Mattie Ross

———

Regardless of which of these character arcs your protagonist (or other cast member) follows, they'll also have a want and a need. This want is the personal desire or goal that they believe will make their life more fulfilling or meaningful—if they can achieve it. This is the motivation that will drive them for much of your story.

Alongside this want is something they need, and this need is the real key to their fulfillment. This need will almost always run counter to their want, and a big part of their character arc will be about learning how to embrace their need while either still achieving their want, or giving it up entirely.

Returning to the examples we used above, Mulan desires validation and Luke craves adventure. However, these wants won't fulfill their character arcs. Rather than basing her self-worth on the opinions of others, Mulan needs to see that her worth is innate and learn to value her cleverness and assertiveness. Likewise, Luke will need to recognize that what started as simply an adventure has become something far greater, and that he has a critical role to play in the salvation of the galaxy.

Of course, at the start of your protagonist's journey they'll still be actively pursuing their want. Their need and the important lesson attached to it won't be within view quite yet.

Fortunately, your protagonist's want is perfect for providing the motivation they need to engage with your story's conflict! Ask yourself:

- What problems does my protagonist have at this stage in their life?
- What about their life makes them uncomfortable or unhappy?
- What do they believe will fix this? (This is their want)
- How can they put that into action through goals?

- How does my story's conflict either disrupt or provide a new avenue to pursue those goals?

By carefully considering what your protagonist desires and how that desire connects to the conflict of your story, you create the perfect recipe for strong motivation. From there, it's simply a matter of putting that motivation into play.

Facing Their Flaws

Of course, another big element of any character's arc is facing their flaws.

Every character—just like anyone you meet—will have a flaw of some kind, and this will be especially true for your protagonist. This is another important element of their personality that you'll want to show off during the early stages of your draft. Their flaws will humanize them, and they're yet one more way to inject conflict into your story.

Ultimately, your protagonist's flaw could be anything, but it doesn't need to be extreme. Instead, their flaw is whatever holds them back from becoming a better, happier person, no matter how subtle.

For instance, Luke's flaw in *A New Hope* is his naïveté. He isn't fully prepared for the danger his adventure will bring and he believes he isn't capable of much. After all, he's just a farm boy. Meanwhile, Mulan's flaw is her struggle to stand up for herself, which connects closely to the conflict between her want and need.

In fact, a character's flaws are often related or even caused by their need. While this isn't a requirement, it's certainly not a bad thing! If you're unsure what flaw fits your protagonist, consider the lesson they need to learn as a part of their character arc. Whatever this lesson is, you can assume their flaw will be the opposite. A character who needs to learn generosity will be greedy, and one who needs self-confidence with start out anxious.

You can show off your protagonist's flaws in a variety of ways, but don't shy away from being subtle. If this flaw is something baked into their personality—which it should be —showing it to your reader is as simple as making your protagonist handle a situation poorly due to that flaw. Rarely does a flaw need to be explicitly spelled out; most readers will catch on!

Preparing for Tomorrow

Once you've started thinking about the best ways to establish your protagonist's desires and flaws, you'll have one final thing to account for: progress.

Before you wrap up your writing for today, you need to put your protagonist's motivation into action. They should be aware of your story's conflict by now, but they may not be ready to engage with that conflict just yet. To help get both them and your plot moving forward, you need to make the case for why they should uproot their normal life and get involved.

This is especially important now, because tomorrow your protagonist will have to make the choice to set out on their adventure—and they'll need to be prepared to make that choice when the opportunity presents itself.

Just like everything else we've discussed today, this will tie in closely to your protagonist's character arc. The way to create forward progress within your plot is to spark tension that motivates your protagonist in a certain direction.

Mulan first faces the conflict of her story when her father is drafted, but that doesn't mean she's ready to make any major leaps or begin her journey. Instead, we get a handful of scenes where Mulan sees the effects this will have on her family.

For starters, her aging father struggles while practicing his swordsmanship, and later her mother and grandmother are visibly distressed. Slowly but surely, these things build in Mulan's mind until she confronts her father. Why does he have to go? He's already served in the army, and to her this means he should stay home, but instead of listening to her fears he silences her. This is the final straw that pushes Mulan to action. She's motivated by a desire to be useful and valuable to her family, and now that she understands the stakes of inaction this motivation kicks into high gear.

Luke's early scenes play out a bit differently. He craves adventure, and when he finds a mysterious plea for help left with an equally mysterious droid, he sets out to learn more. Through this he finds Obi-Wan, a mentor figure that will be with him in one form or another throughout his journey. It's Obi-Wan that encourages Luke to set out on his adventure, telling him tales of Jedi Knights and of his father. Thanks to this coaxing, by the time Luke faces the turning point of his story, he's already come around to the possibility of a true adventure.

So, while establishing your conflict is important, it's equally as important that you show *why* your protagonist feels motivated to get involved. After all, they'll need a good reason to leave their ordinary life behind.

The Goals of Day Two

If all went well, today you continued the momentum you built on Day One, both for your story and yourself.

As I keep reiterating, a lot of this challenge is a mental game, one about keeping yourself motivated despite the rigors of writing thousands of words a day. Your protagonist will need a few shots of motivation as well, especially at this early stage —writers and their characters aren't that different in that regard.

Ultimately, even if this challenge has felt difficult so far, I'm glad you're sticking with it. Today was a particularly long one, and I'll be upfront in warning you that tomorrow will be just as involved. However, things will get smoother as your plot picks up.

There are many more exciting things to explore over the next eight days, so don't stop now!

Tomorrow we'll face the first turning point of your story, but for now, here are the goals you've completed for Day Two:

1. Establish a healthy writing routine that discourages you from listening to your inner editor.
2. Introduce the main conflict of your novel to both your protagonist and reader.
3. Find what motivates your protagonist using their character arc, want, and need.
4. Start showing why your protagonist needs to get involved in the main conflict.

By the end of today, your draft should have approximately eight completed scenes (or ten thousand words) and your protagonist should be ready to begin their journey.

On to Day Three!

4

DAY THREE: THE JOURNEY BEGINS

R emember how, back on Day Zero, I mentioned some days would feature longer, more intense scenes?

Well, this is one of those days.

Today we'll be tackling the first major turning point of your story, called the First Plot Point. Like so much of this early phase of your novel, there's a lot of foundational material to cover, from plot to characters and conflict. After today, your story will be fully in motion, meaning you'll want to take your time to ensure everything is in the right place for the days to come.

We'll also be taking a closer look at your outline for the first time today. You see, up until now everything you've been writing has been more or less straightforward. You introduced your protagonist, set up your conflict, and got your reader introduced to your story's world. From now on, however, you'll need to rely on your outline much more heavily as we dive deeper into the core of your novel.

This is where things get more complex, but don't worry—nothing you'll face today (or any other day for that matter) will be insurmountable!

Using Your Outline

As your story gets more involved over the next few days, you'll inevitably find yourself leaning on your outline more and more. This is the case not only so you know what you'll be writing next, but so you know what you've *already* written.

Here is where your outline really shines, and it's why I encouraged having one to begin with. As your story's conflict gets into full swing, you'll start introducing new settings and characters at a much faster pace, adding a whole slew of additional personalities, worldbuilding, tension, conflicts, and perspectives to your story in the process. The ability to keep track of it all will be tremendously helpful as you continue this challenge.

Specifically, you'll use your outline in a few key ways. You'll use it to:

- Keep track of what scenes you still need to write.
- Work through tricky or challenging scenes.
- Mark changes to your story as you go.
- And keep your inner editor in check.

The first item on this list is the most obvious, and it's likely you've already been using your outline this way. As you go along, you need an easy way to know what still needs writing, along with what's supposed to happen next. Not only does this help you stay on top of your goals, but it makes sure your story is always moving forward, never stagnating at a dead end without you realizing. This is why it's so beneficial to check back with your outline periodically as you write your draft, both to measure your progress and to reorient yourself within your novel.

Alongside this more self-explanatory use, your outline is also a great tool for better understanding your story's scenes, *without* having to spend hours writing and rewriting them.

This is another reason I recommended sketching out your scenes beforehand. Still, even if you did, you're likely to run into a few scenes that stump you in ways you weren't prepared for—such is the life of a writer, after all!

Perhaps your characters aren't behaving as you expected or the plot twist you've been setting up doesn't turn out quite right. In these instances, pull out your outline and take a look at the bigger picture. Where are you in your story's overarching plot, and what major milestone are you building towards next? Once you've taken this into account, you can use your outline to jot down different ideas until you find the solution to your problem.

Your outline is essentially your playground, making it the perfect space for scribbling down notes as you coax your story back into place. From there, you'll just have to look at your next few scenes and make any updates necessary to reflect these changes, before diving back into writing.

Of course, that's not all your outline is good for, and this is where we get into some less intuitive benefits of outlining.

You see, many writers think outlines are a restrictive force, something that prevents them from exercising their creativity as they write. However, this is far from the truth. In reality, your outline is just a guide book, meant to keep you on track—but also to catalog the many changes you'll naturally make to your story as you go.

A big part of this organization is knowing how to turn your outline into a living document, one that grows and evolves as your story does. You should always be taking notes on your story as you write, but this is especially true whenever you make major changes. Personally, I like to do this at the end of each writing session, but you can also mark changes as you go. Just make sure you write down what you changed, and then check your outline to ensure this change won't break any other part of your story down the line.

This is also hugely helpful for keeping your inner editor in check. We've talked a lot about this inner editor so far, and we'll continue to, but this is essentially your real-world writing antagonist. Fortunately, your outline is a great shield against them.

As you write, you'll be able to feel when your inner editor is brewing. Suddenly, there will be a strange sense of pushback against what you're creating and the nagging doubt that your story isn't good enough will surface. However, instead of letting these feelings swamp you, turn to your outline. Pull out a highlighter or colored pen and make a quick note beside whatever scene you're working on. Mention what you're feeling, and why.

Didn't think that character's introduction was any good? That's ok—make a note of it. Don't like how you described that majestic mountain in the distance? No problem—make a note of it.

This way, you're calming your inner editor by taking these potential flaws into account, while simultaneously refusing to give up your momentum. These notes should only ever be shorthand, just quick reminders to revisit later during the editing process. While your outline may fill up with red pen, your draft can remain clean, helping you focus on the task at hand and leave editing until later—where it belongs.

A Note on Research

As you go through and mark up your outline, a specific note you're bound to run into is something along the lines of, "Needs More Research."

It's natural for questions to come up as you work on your first draft, no matter how exhaustive your brainstorming and outlining process was. When you notice these, you may feel inclined to pause and research them. On some level this seems logical—wouldn't it be better to get your facts straight before you continue?

Actually, no.

You see, this can become a huge time sink, and there are far better ways to answer these questions without burning through precious writing time. Personally, I would discourage you from researching at all while writing your first draft, and would instead advise you to keep a dedicated page in your outline full of questions to answer later on. Whenever something comes up, make a note of what it is and where to find it in your story. Alternatively, you can highlight the offending passage in your draft to return to while editing.

In particular, if you run into any specific terms you don't know the word for, just use a random keyword you can swap out later on, once you've decided on the right replacement. The same goes for whenever you're unsure what to name a newly introduced character or location—save the task for another day.

From there, move on.

Don't waste hours in an Internet driven hole, because that's what most research ends up becoming. Research is best done in the outlining phase, and you should save anything you missed for editing. In fact, this may be the best time to research for your novel, since you'll have a more complete and holistic understanding of your final story.

Still, it's possible you'll come across a piece of information that is *truly* critical. As loathe as I am to admit it—because seriously, I've spent almost as much time writing my novels as I've spent wandering the Internet looking up semi-important information like the social hierarchy of rabbits— there are times when research is worthwhile for your first draft. In these instances, at least wait until you've completed your writing goals for the day. Better yet, only allow yourself to sit down and research *if* you hit your goals.

Not only will this prevent you from losing momentum, but it might even give you an extra spike of motivation—if that question really is as important as you think it is!

The Basics of Story Structure

As I mentioned at the start of this chapter, today will be when your story finally reaches its first major turning point: The First Plot Point.

From here, your story will transition into its second act, marking a whole new phase of its plot. The story structure terms below will come up more and more often as a result, so let's quickly cover what everything means to make sure we're on the same page:

- **Act 1 (Setup):** Act 1 comprises the first quarter of your story and is all about preparing your cast for the journey ahead. This is where you'll introduce your setting, protagonist, and the conflict they'll be facing.
- **Act 2 (Confrontation):** Act 2 forms the bulk of your story, around 50%. All the adventures, twists, and turns happen here, giving you time to flesh out your characters, backstories, and settings. Most importantly, Act 2 contains a major turning point where your protagonist shifts from reacting to the conflict to actively trying to resolve it thanks to the new skills and knowledge they've gained thus far.
- **Act 3 (Resolution):** Act 3 is the final quarter of your novel and sees your conflict come to its end. Here your protagonist and antagonist will have their final confrontation. Once you resolve the conflict of your story, you'll have a moment to hint at the future and explain what happens after your protagonist's journey is over (or set up a sequel, if you're planning one).

Within these three acts, there are also six plot points you'll need to keep track of. Fortunately, you already wrote your story's Hook back on Day One, leaving five still to go:

————

The First Plot Point:

This is the moment your story truly begins, as well as the moment when Act 1 ends. Your protagonist has spent Act 1 learning about the conflict they're about to face, and here they'll finally become fully involved in the events of your story thanks to a pivotal decision they'll make.

The Midpoint:

This is the next major turning point of your story. Your Midpoint marks the halfway point of your novel and sees your protagonist face a major challenge. By overcoming this challenge they'll gain new skills or knowledge that will allow them to start actively shaping the events of your story. From here on out, they have a plan for resolving the conflict, even if that plan might fail later.

The Third Plot Point:

This plot point marks the end of Act 2 and is a harsh reality check for your protagonist. Here they'll suffer a major defeat at the hands of your antagonist, throwing their previous plans into disarray. This will be their lowest moment, when they feel like they've lost everything. In the following scenes, they'll need to reflect on their goals in order to recommit to the journey ahead.

The Climax:

This is the final conflict between your protagonist and antagonist. It may be a major battle, a confession of love, or a heated confrontation. Whatever it is, your protagonist will need to draw on all the skills, knowledge, and alliances they've gained throughout your story if they want to succeed. Alternatively, they may fail.

The Resolution:

These are the last few scenes of your story, meant to show your readers the final effects of your Climax. Whether your protagonist succeeded or failed in their quest, here you'll take a moment to say some final goodbyes and show what your story's world will look like going forward. You may also lay the groundwork for sequels here.

―――――

You can see these plot points spread across your novel's three acts in the graph below, with the rising line representing the tension of your story's conflict:

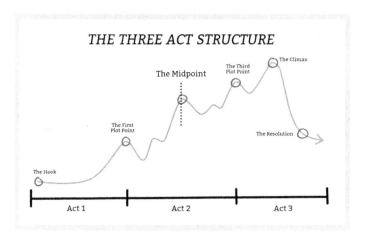

THE THREE ACT STRUCTURE

The Hook

The First Plot Point

The Midpoint

The Third Plot Point

The Climax

The Resolution

Act 1 Act 2 Act 3

Of course, looking at definitions is all well and good, but what do these look like in action? Well, here's the plot of *A New Hope* explained using this structure:

―――――

The Hook:

Darth Vader intercepts Princess Leia's ship in search of stolen plans for the Death Star. However, Princess Leia sneaks them out of his grasp with the help of R2-D2.

The First Plot Point:

Upon returning home with Obi-Wan, Luke finds that Stormtroopers have killed his aunt and uncle. Now with a personal reason to hate the Empire, Luke joins Obi-Wan and the two set out in search of Princess Leia.

The Midpoint:

While searching for Alderaan, a tractor beam pulls the Millennium Falcon aboard the Death Star. They must now escape, made even more complex when they realize Princess Leia is also on board.

The Third Plot Point:

Obi-Wan sacrifices himself in a battle with Darth Vader to buy Luke and his friends enough time to escape the Death Star. Luke is powerless as he watches Darth Vader kill his mentor and his last connection to home.

The Climax:

As the Death Star approaches the Rebel base, Luke and the other Rebel pilots scramble to destroy it. With Han Solo's help and his own trust in the Force, Luke blows up the Death Star.

Unknown to the Rebels, Darth Vader narrowly escapes.

The Resolution:

The movie ends during a large ceremony, with Princess Leia honoring Han and Luke for their role in destroying the Death Star.

We'll be going over all of these plot points as they come up down the road, but this preview should help you keep in mind the long-term trajectory of your story.

Writing the First Plot Point

At this point, your draft should be approaching the First Plot Point. Of everything you write today the First Plot Point will be by far the most involved, as it marks the first major turning point of your novel. This is where your story will really jump into action!

Just like we discussed above, the First Plot Point is where your protagonist becomes fully involved in your story's conflict, marking the moment of no return. Because of this, they'll have to make some sort of decision here, with the result of that decision embroiling them in the conflict from here on out.

Fortunately, since you already know your story's main conflict, you should be fine here. Though the First Plot Point will likely be difficult to write, at its core it's no different from any other scene. The biggest thing you need to keep in mind is to ensure your protagonist is playing an active role in this scene. Even if your story's conflict pushes them in a certain direction, the final choice to take action should be theirs—though it may be subtle.

For instance, a protagonist whose child is missing could always choose to do nothing—or they could try to find them, though this might seem like the only logical decision to you. Inaction is always an option, even when no other options seem to exist, so make it clear that your protagonist is choosing to engage with your story and begin their journey. Otherwise, they lose agency over their adventure and their later victories will feel less meaningful. After all, the choice to engage with change is a powerful one, and your readers will pay attention to it.

Of course, your protagonist will need a good reason to leave the comfort and familiarity of their ordinary world. This is especially true since they'll be exchanging that comfort for the uncertainty of your story's conflict, meaning something will need to spur their decision.

Whether they're searching for someone like in the example above or they've been offered a new job in a faraway city, the reason will be different for every protagonist. However, this reason should always relate back to your story's conflict.

- Luke chooses to leave with Obi-Wan and train as a Jedi after Stormtroopers kill his aunt and uncle.
- Hiccup chooses to learn more about dragons after he shoots down—but fails to kill—a Nightfury.
- Mulan chooses to disguise herself as a man and join the army after her ailing father is drafted.
- Ashitaka chooses to journey west in search of a cure after he is cursed trying to protect his village.

You can see the common pattern here: a character *chooses* to do something *after* something happens that spurs them forward.

All of these characters made a choice, even if circumstances practically forced them to do so. They always had a way out, or at least the option of inaction. Now, however, there will be no turning back.

The Aftermath

Of course, once you write this pivotal scene, you'll be left with a question: turning points are all well and good, but what happens afterwards?

Once the First Plot Point is over and your story officially enters Act 2, you'll have to consider a few new things as you write. Most immediately, you'll need to consider the consequences of your protagonist's choice. What are the stakes here, and what immediate challenges will they face because of their actions?

These stakes may be something your protagonist doesn't even realize, such as in *Mulan*. After Mulan leaves home, we see a short scene where her parents warn us that she'll be killed if the army discovers her true identity. However, Mulan doesn't automatically realize this, but that's ok. The audience is aware of the stakes of her adventure. When these stakes come back to haunt her later on, we're ready for them, lending a sense that the story has come full circle.

Alongside these stakes, you'll want to explore the new, foreign world your protagonist finds themselves in. This "newness" doesn't necessarily mean in the physical sense though. While many protagonists travel to a foreign location as they begin their journey, plenty of others stay home. What makes this an unknown world is that the rules have suddenly changed—whether that's related to a change in location, circumstances, social standing, mindset, or goal.

Ultimately, regardless of whether this is a new world in the physical sense or not, you'll want to explore what makes it different. How have the rules changes?

A great way to show this off is to put your protagonist in a situation where they'll operate under their old assumptions —only to promptly be proven wrong. It makes sense that they wouldn't understand all of these new rules right away, and they'll need time to acclimate to their new situation. Expect them to fail a lot in this early stage of Act 2.

We'll get into more of those failures tomorrow, but for now keep in mind this important shift.

The Goals of Day Three

With Day Three at its end, you've passed the first major turning point of your story—your plot is now underway!

In many ways, this challenge will get harder from here, especially as we start dealing with more complex aspects of your story. On the other hand, it could actually get easier. Getting your novel off the ground is always a challenge, both for your own motivation and because of the actual process of introducing your story to your reader. You should be proud of how far you've come, even in just three short days! While there's still more to write, you're well underway.

Tomorrow we'll begin putting your protagonist to the test, but for now, here are the goals you've completed for Day Three:

1. Mark any changes you've made to your story in your outline—consider making this a regular practice going forward.
2. Create a page in your outline for questions or topics you want to research later.
3. Write your story's First Plot Point, ensuring your

protagonist makes an active choice to begin their journey.

4. Show off the immediate consequences of your protagonist's decision.

By the end of today, your draft should have approximately twelve completed scenes (or fifteen thousand words) and your story's First Plot Point should be complete.

On to Day Four!

5

DAY FOUR: THE TRIALS OF ACT TWO

I f you've ever read a novel that seemed to drag on and on, its second act was likely the culprit. Characters moved from place to place, talked about their plans and intent, and maybe even started a few fights, but nothing felt meaningful —and as a result, nothing felt engaging.

This is the danger of Act 2.

You see, Act 2 is interesting, because it presents something of a dual challenge for both you and your characters. While your cast faces their first set of obstacles here, you'll be facing your own trials, as Act 2 presents unique challenges for us as writers.

This is because Act 2 is by far the largest section of your story, taking up half of your novel's total run time. You'll need to fill that space with something, and deciding what is a difficult task in and of itself. Of course, the difference between just filling it with something and filling it with something *meaningful* is a big one.

You have quite a few scenes to write before you get close to the next turning point of your plot, meaning today you'll want to develop a plan for how you'll handle this open expanse of your story. Fortunately, there are ways to keep Act 2 relevant and meaningful to your larger novel—with a bit of forward planning.

Still, it's easy to get caught up in the monotony and forget what you're working towards over the next handful of scenes. To help mitigate this, we'll be looking at the many ways you can stay inspired, both today and throughout this challenge, along with tricks for keeping your story engaging as you march towards its Midpoint.

Staying Inspired

A major part of staying motivated during this challenge is keeping yourself inspired. When you're brimming with ideas, the challenge of writing thousands of words a day becomes much less burdensome, and perhaps even exciting. However, you can also expect your inspiration to wane as you get deeper into this challenge. Not only are you settling into the routine of writing, but you're constantly needing to come up with new ideas. It stands to reason that your creative mind will get exhausted during this process!

All of this raises the question of what you can do to jumpstart your inspiration when it starts to fade.

We'll be talking about some specific story elements you can use to keep your ideas fresh later today, but there's also a useful tool you yourself can create. This will remain useful regardless of what day of the challenge you're on, and we'll be referencing it often as the days go by.

This tool?

Your collection.

If you've already read *The Ten Day Outline*, you're likely familiar with what I mean by collection (and you're welcome to skip this section if you are). I went into a lot more detail on how to create and use a collection in that book, as it was an integral part of the outlining process. Put short, this collection is a curated museum of inspiring images, music, quotes, and more, all of which relate back to the story you're trying to create. Whenever you feel strapped for ideas, you can return to this collection and browse what's inside, letting its contents do much of the difficult brainstorming for you.

For instance, say you're writing a story that takes place in a massive, endless forest. The trees reach to the sky and block out all but a faint dapple of sunlight, and the animals that live within the forest have evolved in strange ways to compensate. Sounds like a pretty magical place right?

However, as your story goes on you might run out of ways to liven up this location. What more is there to say about this place? What could you introduce to break the monotony of endless tress that won't betray your original idea of an all-consuming forest?

This is where you would turn to your collection.

Inside, you would have a handful of images and videos showcasing different forests, mountains, caves, and tunnels, all of which you could blend into your story to add more interest to your settings. Likewise, if you aren't sure how to describe a scene, you might turn to the music or quotes you added to your collection to recapture the tone of your story. Essentially, this collection serves as your backup plan, a safety net for whenever you're at a loss for words. While your outline is there to guide you as you organize your scenes and create your plot, your collection is there to keep the words flowing and your creativity thriving.

Creating this collection isn't particularly difficult either.

In many ways, it's similar to a mood board, where you collect various images that represent a specific idea, tone, or vision. However, to best serve your novel your collection should go a bit further.

To create your collection, you'll want to start by gathering inspiring material in bulk. Browse the Internet and use search engines like Google or Pinterest to hunt down an assortment of images, music, videos, and quotes that resonate with your story. These should all capture some element of your plot, characters, worldbuilding, or tone.

From there, dump them into one common folder. This is where you'll begin sorting, because each item in your collection should fit a category related to your story. How you sort your personal collection is up to you, but here are some common categories you might consider:

- Settings
- Characters
- Tools and Objects
- Plants and Animals
- Culture

Of course, you could sort these dozens of different ways. For instance, you might create a dedicated folder for each character in your story, rather than lumping them together in a generic "characters" category. You could even add images of rooms or clothing that you feel fit that character's lifestyle or personality.

Regardless of how you sort your personal collection, you should expect that some of the materials you chose won't be as applicable to your novel as you originally thought. This means your next task is to sort through your categories and weed out any items that don't fit your vision for your novel. Each category in your collection should be a bite-sized representation of your story, so be ruthless here.

Finally, with your categories pared down and sorted, your collection is complete. As you can see, this is definitely more intensive than your average mood board, but it serves a similar purpose. Now, whenever you're out of ideas, you can flip through your collection and reconnect with your original vision for your story. When you're at a loss for words, you have a curated wellspring of inspiration to draw from. Sometimes, even something as simple as describing an image from your collection is enough to jog your creativity and get you writing again. As we get deeper into this challenge, having a collection like this will be a big comfort whenever you're feeling stuck.

Working Towards the Midpoint

Of course, there's another equally important side to inspiration, and that's an engaging plot. You won't always be at a loss for words—sometimes it'll be the events of your story that you're struggling how to create.

As I mentioned back at the start of today's chapter, many novels fall into a trap when they reach Act 2. Their authors aren't sure how to keep the story moving in a cohesive way, so they end up adding extraneous scenes to pad out their second act. Essentially, they're wasting time until they're ready to begin the Midpoint, unsure how else to fill the large void between plot points.

It's this void that scares so many writers, though I do know a few who get excited about Act 2 precisely because of this open space. You see, Act 2 is your first chance to dig in deep and begin exploring subplots, side characters, and the wider expanse of your story's world. There's a lot you can write about here, but unlike Act 1 there isn't as much direction on what you *need* to write.

Fortunately, there is more structure than you might see at first glance.

This is because Act 2 is actually split into two halves: Act 2.0 and Act 2.5. The half prior to your Midpoint is Act 2.0, and this phase of your story is all about your characters reacting to their new circumstances after the First Plot Point. They've left their normal world behind and the rules of their life have likewise changed. What they used to take for granted is no longer possible here, and they'll need to adapt and learn quickly if they're to survive their journey.

Act 2.5, on the other hand, focuses on action. Your characters will be much wiser by this point in your novel, along with being better equipped to face your story's conflict. We'll be talking about this second phase of Act 2 in more detail on a later day.

Ultimately, what all this means is that every scene of Act 2.0 needs to connect to your Midpoint in some way. When writing today's scenes, your story's Midpoint should always be on your mind, because you'll need to use your characters' goals to push them towards that next turning point. This is what separates engaging stories from dull ones—every scene has a purpose, and every goal leads to the next.

The Role of Scene Structure

As great as it sounds to make all of your characters' goals and actions meaningful to your larger story, doing so won't necessarily feel intuitive for everyone. You want these goals to feel like they come from a realistic place—otherwise your readers will start to sense your presence as the author in the background of your story.

This is where scene structure comes in.

Scenes, as I've mentioned before, are basically mini stories that build on top of each other to form your novel. What's more, each scene follows a structure very similar to the Three Act Structure, though slightly abbreviated:

- **Goal:** Your characters are pursuing a goal.
- **Challenges:** They face various conflicts while trying to reach that goal.
- **Outcome:** There's an outcome, either positive or negative.
- **Reaction:** Your characters react to that outcome.
- **Reflection:** They consider their options going forward.
- **Decision (New Goal):** They make a decision, forming a new goal and beginning the cycle again.

This six part structure is also split into two different phases: Action and Reaction, just like the two halves of Act 2 (though these are reversed).

The first of these two contains the Goal, Challenges, and Outcome, and is what you would traditionally think of as a scene. This Action phase is all about your characters pursuing their goals, battling their enemies, making allies, and getting into trouble. At the end of this phase, they'll have either achieved their goal, achieved it with unintended consequences, or failed to achieve it at all.

From there the scene moves into the more understated Reaction phase, consisting of Reaction, Reflection, and Decision. While this can be as short as a single sentence or as long as an entire monologue, it's usually a few paragraphs in total. This half of your scene is all about your cast processing what they've just experienced. They'll react to the events of the Action phase, reflect on what that means for them, and then decide on a new goal that will lead into the next scene.

For example, here's the opening scene of Princess Mononoke broken down with this structure:

- **Goal:** A creature is approaching Ashitaka's village, and it's his job to keep an eye on it.
- **Challenges:** As the creature comes into view, he realizes it's a demon. If he touches it he'll be cursed, which becomes a problem when it attacks him and his village.
- **Outcome:** Ashitaka jumps in front of the demon to protect three girls from his village. He's able to kill the creature, but it curses him in the process.
- **Reaction:** Ashitaka is in tremendous pain. He and others from his village struggle to heal the wound in whatever way they can.
- **Reflection:** As it lays dying, the demon warns the villagers and Ashitaka that they'll suffer thanks to its hatred and grief. Ashitaka is afraid, and will need the support of his community to figure out his next steps.
- **Decision:** Ashitaka will consult with the elders of his village to see if there is any way to undo the curse.

The next scene begins as you'd expect—with Ashitaka meeting with the leaders of his village, searching for a way to heal this unnatural wound.

While you shouldn't stress over scene structure too much when writing your first draft, understanding this basic chain of events is a great way to build further scenes using the ones you already have. Since every scene begins with one goal and ends with the next, you can create a seamless chain of events leading towards your Midpoint. This is the real value of scene structure—not only does it keep your scenes organized, but it gives you a template for creating a natural flow of events. Every beat of your novel connects to the larger plot, and as a result, nothing feels extraneous or wasted.

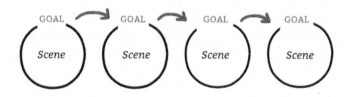

However, even with a strong understanding of scene structure you may lose track of your characters' goals, especially if you didn't outline your scenes before beginning this challenge. In that instance, it can be helpful to create a short list of your scene goals leading towards the Midpoint.

This doesn't need to take long, and is as simple as looking at each scene and seeing how its outcome affects the beginning of the next. Based on these observations, write down your characters' goals for those scenes. Now, as you work on your goals for today, you can reference this list to plan for whatever scene is coming up next.

Importantly, this method will work for your subplots as well. Act 2.0 is when you'll get your first chance to explore your story's subplots in depth and, just like your main plot, each scene of your subplots needs to be connected. Though these subplot scenes may be scattered throughout the various scenes of your main plot, you can still use this same scene structure and goal system to tie your subplots together.

Challenges for Your Cast

A big part of moving your story's plot forward during Act 2.0 is challenging your cast, and this is especially true for your protagonist. This is the tests and trials phase of their character arc, meaning your goal is to push them to grow and confront their inner struggle at every turn. Luckily, much like connecting your scenes this doesn't have to be as hard as it seems.

At its core, forcing your protagonist to grow as a character is really about teaching them a lesson. If you remember from back on Day Two, your protagonist needs something in order to finally overcome their inner struggle, but they don't know it yet. Now is your chance to force them to recognize they have a problem by setting them up against challenges you know they'll fail at. Slowly but surely these failures will make it clear that they need to change if they're to get what they want, and as the stakes of your story increase so too will the realization that they need to grow as a character.

If you're familiar with many action movies, this period of realization is often shown as a montage, following the protagonist as they begin their training, fail repeatedly, and finally learn how to stand on their own two feet. The montage then ends with a victory they only earn thanks to their growth as a character, preparing them for the bigger turning point they'll face at the Midpoint.

In fact, this is exactly how Act 2.0 of *Mulan* plays out. While there are a few scenes that set up her new world and introduce us to the characters she'll be fighting alongside, the rest of her Act 2.0 features a musical number. Here she trains, falls down a lot, and is finally kicked out of the army for good. For all intents and purposes, she has failed to adapt to this new world, and it's clear her lack of physical strength is why. However, before she leaves she has an epiphany— why approach everything like the other soldiers when she can bring her own unique skills to the table?

Thanks to this realization, Mulan not only proves her worth through her cleverness, but finally gains the acceptance of her fellow soldiers as well. This lesson on self-worth is one Mulan will continue to struggle with throughout her story, but this turning point marks the first time she puts it into action, and it'll only build from here.

Of course, it's unlikely a montage like this one will make sense for your novel. They're perfect for the shorter runtimes of movies, but novels—well, not so much.

Still, you can apply these same principles to your story. Simply set your character up against a variety of challenges you know they'll fail at, building until they finally begin to embrace the lesson of their character arc.

Sample Scenes:

Despite how straightforward these structures and arcs may seem on paper, I don't want to discount how complex they can feel when you sit down to write them. Thinking of ways to challenge your characters can cause a lot of stress for many writers, even when they have a clear Midpoint to work towards.

Fortunately, there are some common scenes many stories share in their second act. While you by no means have to use these scenes, they can be a great way to jog your inspiration and find new ways to test your cast.

Here are ten to consider:

———

A New Situation:

Immediately after the First Plot Point, your protagonist will enter a new world. This could literally involve them traveling to a new location, or it could simply be a major change to their normal, everyday life. Either way, they'll need some time to process this change and observe what's different about their newfound situation.

Learning the Rules:

In any new situation there will be new rules and your cast, especially your protagonist, will need to learn about these rules. Often, they'll only learn through failure or by accidentally bringing on the ire of whoever enforces these rules in their new world.

The Watering Hole:

In many stories, the protagonist and their allies will meet at a central gathering place upon entering their new world. Think of the Cantina in *A New Hope* or the local saloon in nearly every classic western movie. This is a great chance to introduce a large group of new characters, and often involves a mentor figure guiding the protagonist as they figure out how to blend into this unknown crowd.

Making Plans:

While Act 2.0 is mostly about your protagonist reacting to their new environment, that doesn't mean they won't have goals and plans to pursue. Even as they struggle to get their feet under them, they'll be trying to find ways to resolve the conflict they're facing, making this a great time to meet with their allies and develop a plan of attack.

Tests, Challenges, and Allies:

As we've talked about throughout today's chapter, Act 2.0 is all about tests and trials. Because of this, make sure your story includes scenes where your protagonist faces tests of their new skills, their ability to adapt, and their knowledge. Through this process they'll often gain allies, learn new things about this strange world, and hopefully learn more about what they're capable of as well.

The Antagonist's Power:

As your protagonist is learning the ropes, your antagonist will be making their own plans. So, in order to keep the stakes of your story in the forefront of your readers' and protagonist's minds, you'll want to include at least one scene where your antagonist's power is made clear.

How can they threaten your protagonist?

This doesn't require them to be physically present in the scene, though they certainly can be. Instead, you simply need to make their power and the danger they pose obvious to your cast.

Meeting with the Goddess:

This is a popular scene within Joseph Campbell's Hero's Journey, and it slots perfectly within Act 2.0. At its core, Meeting with the Goddess is about confronting an explicitly spiritual figure, or at least a mentor with some deeper guidance to offer. This is a chance for your protagonist to witness the power of good, or whatever power opposes your antagonist. While "the dark side" is strong, there's a light side too, and this is its chance to show itself.

Temptation:

Your protagonist will deal with a lot of new things during this phase of their journey, and your story will be pushing hard for them to grow and improve. However, all of this pressure means they're likely vulnerable to temptation.

Many stories choose to tempt their protagonists during Act 2.0 in hopes of weakening their resolve and causing setbacks to their character arcs. For instance, an offer of countless riches in exchange for betraying a new ally might tempt a protagonist who is slowly overcoming their greed. Do they give in, or are they strong enough to resist? That's up to you.

Reorganization:

Whether or not they're tempted, Act 2.0 will definitely feature setbacks for your protagonist—in a section so focused on trials and challenges, that's to be expected.

This means your protagonist will need a chance to meet up with their allies and reorganize their plans, especially as they get closer to the Midpoint. This is a great chance for them to reflect on their experiences so far and show off some of the growth they've gone through during this portion of their journey.

Threshold Guardians:

Right before the Midpoint, your protagonist will likely face what Joseph Campbell calls a Threshold Guardian—these are the forces that try to stop your character from moving forward and entering the Midpoint.

Whether they're an enemy, a supposed ally, a massive storm, a literal gatekeeper, or the protagonist's own inner conflict is up to you and your story. Regardless of how they manifest, these guardians are there as a final test of the protagonist's growth before they can move forward towards the next major turning point of their journey.

———

Again, none of these are requirements by any means— instead, they're simply a way to inspire you as you write, much like the collection you created earlier today. With these tools in hand, you should be well equipped to handle anything Act 2 has to throw at you!

The Goals of Day Four

As I'm sure you've realized by now, today was all about building safety nets you can use as we move into more difficult portions of your draft.

Your collection is there to keep your inspiration flowing, while scene structure can act as a more analytical tool for building cohesive scenes. Understanding how to challenge your characters will keep your story feeling meaningful, while the list of scene ideas are a final guard against getting stuck. Combined, these tools should help you ensure your draft is in good shape by the end of today—and that you are as well.

Of course, it's possible you won't feel compelled to use any of these tools, at least not yet, and that's perfectly fine! If the words keep flowing and your story continues to jump onto the page, that's a wonderful thing, and there's no reason to interrupt a process that's working for you.

Instead, keep these in your back pocket as fail-safes for the days you don't feel quite so confident. There will come a time during this challenge when you're simply unsure how to continue, and having these tools lying in wait gives you the security of knowing you can handle anything your draft throws at you.

Tomorrow we'll cross the halfway mark of your story, but for now, here are the goals you've completed for Day Four:

1. Create a collection for whenever you need a boost of inspiration.
2. List the goals of your cast leading into the Midpoint and use these as a reference while writing.
3. Challenge your characters in meaningful ways, specifically focusing on how these challenges push them to confront their inner struggles.
4. If needed, incorporate common scene types into your story to keep your plot moving forward.

By the end of today, your draft should have approximately sixteen completed scenes (or twenty thousand words) and you should be approaching the Midpoint of your story.

On to Day Five!

6

DAY FIVE: HALFWAY DAY

B y this point in the challenge, you've accomplished a lot. Your story is well underway, your characters are growing and learning, and your plot is about to reach its biggest turning point yet. Personally, I would consider this cause to celebrate, perhaps with a bowl of ice cream and a few episodes of M*A*S*H—though you're welcome to swap in your own vices if you'd prefer.

Of course, we do have a few goals to take care of first.

As I've alluded to in previous chapters, Day Five is where your story will take its next major turn, and this will be the focus of your goals for today. By the end of Day Five, you'll want to have written your Midpoint and set up the next phase of your story. Unfortunately, even compared to the First Plot Point, the Midpoint can be complex.

To help get you past this mid-challenge hump, today we'll talk about how to tackle your story's Midpoint and all the unique challenges that come with it. Along the way we'll connect the many threads of your story, so that by the end of today you'll have earned that pint of ice cream I know you're now dreaming about!

The Purpose of the Midpoint

Thus far, each day of this challenge has opened with tips for handling your mindset as a writer. Today will be a little different—instead of starting with mindset, we'll close with it, meaning it's time to dive headfirst into writing your Midpoint.

Of course, before writing your Midpoint you need to know what role it serves in your story. Back on Day Three we defined the Midpoint as:

- **The Midpoint:** This is the next major turning point of your story. Your Midpoint marks the halfway point of your novel and sees your protagonist face a major challenge. By overcoming this challenge they'll gain new skills or knowledge that will allow them to start actively shaping the events of your story. From here on out, they have a plan for resolving the conflict, even if that plan might fail later.

As you can hopefully tell from this definition, your Midpoint is all about setting up the shift from the reactive phase of Act 2.0 into the active phase of Act 2.5. It's very similar to the First Plot Point in that regard—though it also serves a few specialized functions all its own.

You see, your Midpoint is the next major confrontation your protagonist will face, making it a critical moment in the conflict of your story. This scene will also act as a preview for your Climax, and the skills and abilities your cast gains here should hint at how they'll ultimately handle your finale.

For instance, the Midpoint of *How to Train Your Dragon* follows Hiccup on his very first flight with Toothless, the dragon he found back during the First Plot Point. Throughout Act 2.0, Hiccup has been struggling to learn more about Toothless, and as part of that effort he's developed a prosthetic tail fin to replace the one Toothless broke when he was captured. The Midpoint is the moment he finally gets to try out this invention, and it's a wild success. Not only is Toothless able to fly again, but Hiccup proves his theories right. What's more, the prosthetic requires Hiccup's help to work, making the two largely dependent from here on out.

This joyous flying scene will be mirrored during the movie's Climax, albeit with a darker tone. Neither Hiccup nor Toothless will be able to resolve the conflict without the other's help, forcing them to take flight together. The obstacle course they face during the Midpoint will even echo in the complex flying maneuvers they pull off here. Ultimately, the Climax of the movie becomes infinitely stronger thanks to the groundwork laid by the Midpoint.

However, this is only half of the Midpoint's role.

While the Midpoint is an important turning point for your plot, it's an equally important turning point for your protagonist as well. Your protagonist needs to gain something here, whether that be achieving a major goal or earning new skills, allies, or knowledge.

In Hiccup's case, he gains a new direction that will carry him through the rest of the movie. Toothless has proved to him that the Vikings were wrong about dragons, and from here on out he'll put a plan in place to change their minds. This also ties in closely with his character arc. Throughout the movie Hiccup has struggled to live up to the "Viking ideal," but after realizing the Vikings are wrong about dragons, he's left to wonder what else they may be wrong about. From the Midpoint onward, Hiccup will begin to value his own ideas and unique skills more and more, something he's never done before. While he certainly has a long way to go before completing his character arc, the Midpoint is a major stepping stone on that path.

So, when looked at as a whole, your Midpoint needs to serve a few purposes:

- Your Midpoint should raise the stakes of your story's conflict by introducing a new element or risk.
- It should act as foreshadowing for the Climax.
- It should serve as a turning point within your plot, giving your protagonist the tools they need to actively pursue the conflict.
- It should mark a turning point within your protagonist's character arc, helping them embrace their truth for the first time.

When combined, these elements create a pretty significant moment for your story, all wrapped up in a single scene. You can probably see why the Midpoint is so intimidating for many writers as a result. However, when you think of these four aspects separately, it should become easier to process.

As you write your Midpoint, you simply need to ask yourself:

- What new risks could this scene introduce to raise the stakes of my story?
- How will this change my story's plot going forward?
- Can this scene hint at or mirror my Climax?

- How will this push my protagonist closer to resolving their inner struggles?

What About Secondary Characters?

Of course, as you work on your Midpoint you may wonder: "What about my secondary characters? My protagonist is at a turning point, but what about the rest of my cast?"

Well, I'm happy to say your instinct is right!

If possible, you want all of your major characters to serve a role in this portion of your story. However, unlike with your protagonist, which secondary characters to include and which not to is less cut and dry. No matter what kind of story you're writing, your protagonist always needs to be an active player in the Midpoint, yet that's not always the case for your other cast members.

As we talked about above, *How to Train Your Dragon's* Midpoint only features Hiccup and Toothless, but that makes sense for that movie. The relationship between those two is the focal point of the story, so the Midpoint doesn't lose anything by lacking other characters. In a story with a more involved cast like *A New Hope*, this is less likely to be true— and notice how Han Solo, Chewie, Luke, Leia, and Obi-Wan all play major roles in that movie's Midpoint!

So, if your secondary characters' journeys are just as important to your story as your protagonist's, then you'll want them to be present and active during this scene. This is especially true if they have character arcs of their own (though not all secondary characters need fully fledged arcs).

Still, at the end of the day it's not worth forcing secondary characters into your Midpoint if they don't have a logical reason to be there. If your wider cast fits naturally into the events of this scene, make every effort to include them. If not, you can safely save their personal turning points for later in your story.

Taking Your Time

Finally, once you've finished writing your Midpoint, what comes next? Where does your cast go from here?

This is why it's important to remember that the purpose of the Midpoint is to shift your cast from reaction to action. Previously, they've just been trying to keep up and learn along the way. After your Midpoint though, they should have gained the confidence and knowledge needed to take a more active role in resolving your story's conflict—after all, that's what makes the Midpoint such an important part of your plot to begin with!

So, as you help your cast wind down after the Midpoint, take some time to showcase everything they've learned. How has their victory changed the game? What do they have now that they didn't have before? Above all, how will they change their goals in response?

This might also be a great time for your protagonist to reassess their wants and desires. A lot has happened since their journey began, and their thoughts on themselves and the world are probably beginning to change. It's well worth taking a bit of time to illustrate that here.

Of course, writing your Midpoint is a tall order in and of itself.

Up until now, a big part of this challenge has been writing as much as you can as quickly as you can. As I've said over and over thus far, your first draft isn't the place to worry about prose and polish—instead, it's just here to get your story on paper. You'll come back later on to edit in the fine details and gentle curves that will turn it into a proper novel, but none of that can happen without this foundation to work from.

However, by this point in the challenge you're probably beginning to feel yourself slowing down. While everyone handles the workload that comes with writing a novel differently, you've been working incredibly hard the last few days. It's normal to feel exhausted at this point. We'll talk more about handling this creeping burnout tomorrow, but in the meantime you still need to push through today.

Fortunately, the Midpoint is an excellent tool for breaking through your exhaustion.

A lot of this will be a mental game, but hear me out. Not only is your Midpoint the halfway mark of your story, but it's usually a major event within your plot. Perhaps two characters whose tensions have been brewing will finally confront one another, all of their pent-up emotions spilling into the open. Maybe your hero has been building a team to march into battle with and finally puts them to the test. Or perhaps your protagonist is lost in the wilderness and has an emotional scene where he finally accepts that this wild landscape is his new home.

Whatever the turning point of your story is, it'll probably be an impactful scene filled with energy—and your characters aren't the only ones who can tap into that.

Before you sit down to write today, picture your Midpoint in your head and let it play out behind your eyelids. How is your cast feeling? How are you feeling? Is there wind on your face, the shouts of battle in your ears, or the feeling of your characters standing shoulder to shoulder beside you?

By sinking your teeth into the physical sights, sounds, and feelings of your Midpoint, you can use that energy and excitement to propel yourself through any exhaustion you may be feeling, and hopefully enjoy yourself along the way!

Of course, everyone will feel this energy differently.

For some writers, the Midpoint will give them a second wind, helping them write with the same vigor they had back on Day One. Yet, others will feel called to take their time and immerse themselves in this scene. Even though the first draft isn't the place for polish or prose, it can feel good to indulge in flashier, fancier writing from time to time. This is doubly true when dealing with the intense emotions your cast will be feeling in this scene.

As a result, today is one of the few days where I don't want you to worry about your normal goals. Don't fret about writing four scenes or five thousand words—instead, your only goal is to write the Midpoint from start to finish. Everything else can wait until tomorrow.

The Goals of Day Five

Ultimately, by the end of today your Midpoint will probably be your longest scene to date. There's a lot to deal with when writing the Midpoint, but I hope you were able see past this difficulty and enjoy yourself regardless.

At the end of the day, the Midpoint is just two parts: a turning point for your plot, and one for your protagonist.

If you can nail those two elements, then you'll have nothing to worry about in the days to come. Tomorrow you can pick back up with your normal goals, but for now just focus on this one scene. After all, once it's complete you'll officially be halfway done with your draft, and that's worthy of whatever personal celebration you can come up with!

Tomorrow we'll transition into the next phase of your story, but for now, here are the goals you've completed for Day Five:

1. Write your story's Midpoint, paying special attention to how it shifts your cast from reaction to action.

By the end of today, your draft should have approximately twenty completed scenes (or twenty five thousand words) and your story's Midpoint should be complete.

On to Day Six!

7

DAY SIX: FIGHTING BURNOUT

W e've all felt it before. No matter how much we sleep in, we're still tired. When writing time rolls around we suddenly need to do the dishes, walk the dog, or water the household plants—basically anything other than writing. Even worse, we no longer daydream about our stories before bed, and when we stare at the blinking cursor on our screens few if any words come to us.

We've burnt out.

With the Midpoint finally behind you and the open expanse of Act 2 hovering over your head, this feeling of burnout is no surprise. This is even more true if you're behind on some of your goals, and doubly so if you're still working on the tail end of the Midpoint.

However, I'm here to tell you that this is ok.

This low point is a natural part of this challenge, one almost everyone will face. You've been working incredibly hard the last few days, and by now you're bound to slow down. Instead of giving in to this burnout though, we're going to power through. You see, in many ways this feeling is a lot like running—running is often downright unpleasant until, out of nowhere, you hit a runner's high. Suddenly, your body finds its rhythm and the strain of running fades into the background.

Today, our goal will be to discover your own runner's high. Whether you're barely holding on or are still going strong, the tips below should be the kick you need to find your rhythm again.

Staying in the Groove

By now, I imagine you've developed a strong writing routine —and whether you write in fifteen minute bursts throughout the day or from four to eight at your local library, this routine is definitely a good thing. However, just like your cast reached a turning point yesterday, you've reached a turning point in your own writing.

It's time to mix things up!

For starters, now is the perfect time to reassess your goals and refresh your plans going forward. You're halfway through the challenge, meaning a big portion of the work is behind you, yet there's still plenty to accomplish. To make the rest of this challenge easier, take some time to pull out your calendar and look at your goals thus far:

- Have your goals taken you longer than expected?
- Has your schedule changed, making days you previously planned to write no longer realistic?
- Are you behind on any goals?
- How can you make this challenge easier for yourself, while still making regular progress?

Whatever your situation may be, think carefully about your plans and make any changes you need. This way you can still move full steam ahead, while simultaneously taking into consideration how well this challenge has been going and what time and resources you need to do your best.

From there, the next best thing for handling this sense of burnout is changing up your writing routine.

Just like having oatmeal every day for months will get old— no matter how much you really like it—writing in the same place at the same time with the same sights and sounds will definitely eventually wear thin. Your routine needs to remain interesting, and you need ways to keep your mind stimulated so it doesn't fall into rote repetition.

Early in the challenge, establishing a consistent writing routine was an important part of getting into the habit of writing, but now that's less of the case. You've proven you're dedicated to this challenge, and you're likely comfortable with your habits. All of this opens up the possibility of tweaking various aspects of your routine to help keep things fresh.

Here are some tactics to consider when looking at ways to inject a bit of newness into your writing routine:

————

Find a New Location:

Probably the easiest thing you can do to refresh your routine is to write in a new location. If you've been writing from a home office, move to a new room in your house, write outside, or go to a nearby cafe. If you're already working from outside your home, perhaps a different venue is in order. No matter where you go, the ultimate goal here is to keep your mind stimulated with new sights and sound, in turn keeping your writing fresh and your mind active.

Try a New Style:

Of course, it's not always possible to change your writing location for a variety of reasons. However, you can always mix up your writing style.

Again, this will largely depend on how you've been writing up until now. For instance, if you've been writing in large, two hour blocks, throwing in some burst writing might help. With this format you write for fifteen minutes, break for five, and repeat. On the other hand, if you're already writing in smaller chunks, it could be helpful to mix up the length of either your writing time or your breaks, depending on your preferences.

Use Your Outlet:

Another great way to keep your mind active is actually something we discussed all the way back on Day Zero—your outlets.

Before this challenge even began, I encouraged you to pick one or two outlets like running or cleaning, basically anything that would allow your mind to rest without distractions (meaning no TV). If you haven't been using these outlets so far, I encourage you to start doing so now. While you'll occassionally have to push through a tough part of your draft, there's always something to be said for giving your mind a moment to rest and recoup.

Change Your Inspiration:

Of course, it may not be your mind that's getting stale, but your inspiration. After six days of listening to the same music, looking at the same pictures, and working on the same story, you're bound to start getting tired of it.

This means that now a great time to create a new playlist for your writing sessions, using music better tailored to this next phase of your story! You could even consider seeking out new images, quotes, or music clips to add to your collection, specifically ones that capture the tone of this second half of your novel. And remember—try to finish each writing session when you're still full of ideas, so you'll always have something to pick back up on the next day.

Reward Yourself:

While it can feel weird to train yourself the same way you might train the family dog, we really are just animals at our core—and who doesn't love treats?

So, set smaller goals for yourself that you can achieve throughout your writing sessions, and then don't be shy with the rewards. You may do a happy dance every time you finish writing a scene, or perhaps you let yourself have a piece of candy after every hour of writing. These silly rewards have been helping motivate university students for ages, so it just might work for you too!

Take a Break:

Finally, sometimes you just need a break. The human mind is a muscle, and muscles can only work so hard before they give out. We built in mercy days at the beginning of this challenge for a reason, and if you haven't taken advantage of them yet it may be worth giving yourself permission to have a day off. Rest, relax, and don't even think about your draft for a day. The next morning you can return to writing refreshed and energized, and I'm confident you'll feel much better as a result.

———

None of these are required by any means, but they're still well worth considering if your writing is starting to feel stale. Mix and match them, use some but not others, or try them all! Whatever makes the most sense for you and your personal writing routine.

Starting Their Pursuit

Once your mind is in a better place, it's time to return to your story—and in the aftermath of the Midpoint there's plenty to do.

For starters, you'll want to show the consequences of your Midpoint, both good and bad. These consequences can include any new skills or knowledge your cast has gained, any immediate changes to the conflict of your story, and any new locations, plans, events, or risks that have appeared. Basically, after such a major turning point you're bound to have a few new things to examine and introduce, and you'll want to do that here.

From there, you can shift towards your more long-term goals for the rest of Act 2.5.

During the Midpoint, your protagonist and their allies should have gained new skills and knowledge, meaning they'll also have a new outlook on their previous plans. This makes now the perfect time for everyone to regroup, taking any new information they've learned into account.

Remember, this is when your cast starts taking a more active role in determining the outcome of your story. Let your protagonist and their allies determine how they'll pursue the conflict going forward, and don't be afraid to let them push back against the antagonist's power or even against each other.

This also ties into another thing you need to consider during this phase of your story. Your antagonist likely just received a major blow to their power, and even if your Midpoint didn't directly involve them (such as in *Mulan*) your protagonist still earned a major victory. This shifts the balance of power within your conflict, meaning your protagonist and their allies should enjoy a few more successes than they did in Act 2.0. Whereas before they were struggling to adapt to a new world, now they have their feet planted firmly beneath them, giving them a chance to march forward with renewed confidence.

Long story short, as you move into today's scenes, don't shy away from giving your cast some well-earned victories as they pursue their new goals. They should still face challenges, but they'll be much better equipped to deal with these challenges than before.

Forward, March!

One of the many aspects that makes this portion of your draft so difficult to write is the fact that you're transitioning into a section of your story that largely mirrors one you previously faced.

Just like you wanted to keep the Midpoint in mind while writing Act 2.0, you'll want to bring your Climax to the forefront when writing Act 2.5. This is the next major confrontation of your story (other than a setback we'll deal with soon), and will be where you bring the conflict of your novel to its close. This means every one of your cast's goals and every scene in your story should move towards the

Climax in a meaningful way, preparing your characters for the final showdown.

Of course, you may have started exploring subplots and side stories during Act 2.0, so don't think I'm telling you to neglect those! Instead, you'll just need to think about how these subplots will eventually wrap up. While there's certainly more to explore in your story, by keeping your Climax in mind you won't meander down too many rabbit trails and drag your work out unnecessarily.

You'll also want to keep your characters' inner journeys in mind alongside your Climax. This is especially true where your protagonist is concerned, so think carefully about how they're using their newfound knowledge and growth at this point in your story.

For instance, we talked yesterday about Hiccup's Midpoint in *How to Train Your Dragon*, and from here on out his inner struggle will take on a new form—before he was trying to live up to his society's expectations, but now he wants to change those expectations. Still, his core problem remains. Hiccup will continue to base his self-worth on others' view of him for quite a few more scenes, rather than embracing his innate value the way he needs to. As a result, he'll be in for a painful surprise later on when he finds the other Vikings won't change their minds as easily as he'd hoped. Until he confronts his inner struggle and completes his character arc, this need for others' approval will always haunt him.

This should be true for your protagonist as well.

Whatever inner struggle they suffer from, they'll be one step closer to finally recognizing it after the Midpoint. Yet, there will still be a core piece of the puzzle missing, something that will hold them back from fully embracing their truth and completing their growth.

As I've hinted at previously, these struggles will all come to a head during a major setback before the Climax. We'll talk more about that upcoming scene later on, but for now just keep in mind that not all is as well as it seems. Even though your cast has a new leg up in the conflict, there's still a weakness lingering in the background that will come back to bite them soon.

Avoiding Repetition

If you're thinking this all sounds a lot like Act 2.0, you're right—and this presents some unfortunate problems.

You see, you want to avoid letting this second half of your story become a beat by beat repeat of the first. Act 2.5 is in many ways a mirror of Act 2.0, and many writers struggle to mix things up as a result. This is especially damaging for their stories because Act 2.5 and Act 2.0 are only alike on the surface. When you dig deeper, there are some important differences you'll need to understand.

For starters, this second phase of your novel should see your cast actively dictating how your story progresses from here on out, no longer simply reacting to outside forces. Instead, they need to be making plans, driving the antagonist on the run, and purposefully deciding how to proceed. This is their best chance to show off everything they've learned thus far in your story.

This active phase is also when you should begin raising the stakes and making your novel's conflict more serious. The closer your cast gets to the Climax, the more the tension of your story should build, and increased risk is a reliable way to do that.

For example, the stakes of the original *Star Wars* trilogy slowly shift from Luke and his friends being in danger in the first film, to the entire galaxy hanging in the balance by the end. While the galaxy was at risk all along, this started as an almost peripheral concern for Luke. His immediate quest was more vital, and the long-term plans of the Emperor were still in the distant future. However, as he shifted into a more active role during the second movie, this larger threat became more real and urgent.

A similar transition should begin to happen here for your own story.

Interestingly, this is important not only for your novel itself, but for you as well. If you simply repeated the scenes and conflicts you already covered back on Days Three and Four, you would be bound to get bored with your own story. By raising the stakes, you not only add tension for your characters, but give yourself new ways to up the ante and create original story beats. After all, there's a lot to explore during this phase of your story, so long as you keep things fresh!

The Goals of Day Six

As with so many things in life, boredom is often our greatest enemy—and that's especially true when you throw an overwhelming task into the mix.

I hope the tips the tricks we looked at today help you rest and refresh your mind, especially now that much of the hard work is behind you. Don't hesitate to take a day off if you need it, and do everything you can to take care of both your writing goals and your mind. After all, the key to this challenge really is about mindset. So long as you stay healthy, happy, and inspired, you'll be able to handle everything we face in the coming days!

Tomorrow we'll feel a strange sense of deja vu, but for now, here are the goals you've completed for Day Six:

1. Create a plan to address burnout, and then put that plan into action.
2. Consider the new skills and knowledge your cast has gained and how these will contribute to some well-earned victories.
3. Bring your cast together to reassess their goals and formulate a new plan of action.
4. Remember: while this second phase of your novel may *feel* a lot like the first, there are fundamental differences to keep in mind.

By the end of today, your draft should have approximately twenty four completed scenes (or thirty thousand words) and be well into Act 2.5.

On to Day Seven!

8

DAY SEVEN: WRITER'S DEJA VU

Almost all of us will experience deja vu at some point in our lives. Whether it's the smell of sugar cookies wafting over from across the street or the weird shape of a certain room, the feeling that you've been somewhere before can be a haunting one.

If you happen to be one of the lucky ones unfamiliar with this strange sensation, deja vu is the sense of having been somewhere before, despite that not being the case. Unlike smells, sounds, or places that dig up long lost memories, deja vu happens with things you have no prior experience with—meaning there's no better way to describe this stage of your draft.

You see, by Day Seven you should be well into Act 2.5 of your story and, despite covering new ground for both your novel and your cast, it'll probably feel very familiar to you. Many of the challenges you faced and things you wrote about back on Day Four will come back for a visit today, each with their own new twists. You'll even find a topic from earlier in the challenge making a guest appearance!

So, much like yesterday, today is all about keeping your mind active, finding inspiration wherever you can, and continuing the slow march towards the finale of your story—hopefully without too strong a sense of deja vu.

Keeping Your Words Fresh

As I mentioned, Day Seven brings with it a lot of familiar challenges from Day Four. You're deep into the second half of your story and your plot is slowly moving forward. Just like on Day Four, it'll be easy to get distracted or stalled out here, meaning an important part of today's goals will be keeping your ideas fresh and your story moving.

Just like we talked about back on Day Four, when faced with the large open expanses of Act 2, you'll want to use your characters' goals as a guiding force. Even as we get deeper into your draft, your characters' goals should continue to form a seamless chain of scenes leading towards your story's next major turning point, in this case your Climax. These should be based on the principles of scene structure we discussed earlier on.

Hopefully you've already been putting these structures to work for your story, however, even if you have it can be easy to lose the chain after your Midpoint.

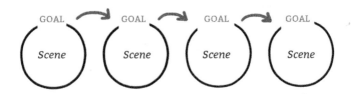

As a result, it's well worth your time to sit down before writing today and sketch out a new list of goals for your cast. Focus specifically on how these goals will lead them towards the Climax of your story, and then think of specific ways these goals could manifest in your scenes.

This is where your collection and your outline will continue to show their value, with each serving a distinct purpose—your outline is the more analytical, organized way of looking at your story, while your collection is all about feeding your imagination and sparking new ideas. As you write your list of character goals, both tools can help you solve some of the problems you might face. For instance, if you're unsure how your characters' goals will fit into the larger plot of your story, reference your outline. On the other hand, if you don't know how to bring those goals to life as scenes, your collection is where you should turn. Which you lean on most heavily will just depend on what you need at that moment.

Still, these tools alone may not be enough to truly get into the minds of your cast. As has been the case throughout this challenge, that role is best served by some intensive brainstorming.

Now is a great time to pause for ten or fifteen minutes and brainstorm the next handful of scenes you'll write. Focus specifically on what your cast is thinking and feeling at this stage of their journey by asking them a few questions:

- What do you still want to achieve?
- What are you afraid might happen?
- What are you hopeful for?
- What have you learned or gained so far?
- Who do you trust and who are you skeptical of?
- What do you think will happen next?

- What do you plan to do about it?
- How do you feel at this moment?

Remember, you're the one asking your cast these questions, but you're not the one providing the answers. It's likely your cast won't know everything about their own story—when you ask them what will happen next their answer may be entirely wrong, even though *you* know the real answer!

Instead, this exercise is about tapping into your cast's mind (especially your protagonist's) in order to get a better idea of how they'll behave after the major changes caused by the Midpoint.

A lot of being a storyteller is about understanding human psychology and the minds of your characters. By thinking through these questions now, you can not only keep your story moving in a compelling way, but you can keep your writing from becoming stale—after all, humans are never as predictable as we might think, and your characters are no exception.

Sample Scenes 2.0

Once you have a strong idea of what goals your cast will pursue at this point in your story, you can start bringing those goals to life through your scenes. Of course, like so much of today this process will feel a lot like it did back on Day Four, meaning you may not be sure exactly how to flesh out your upcoming scenes.

So, to build on the list of sample scenes we created earlier, here are twelve common scenes found in this second phase of many popular stories:

A Quiet Moment:

Immediately after the Midpoint, your protagonist will need a chance to recover. This scene will be a solitary moment for your protagonist, a time for them to reflect on everything that's happened so far along their journey. They're no doubt feeling a lot of new emotions and looking at the world in new ways, making this is the perfect time to explore those changes.

The Fruits of Victory:

Of course, the rest of your cast wants in on the fun too! After the Midpoint, your cast deserves to celebrate and share their victory. Whether they regroup over a large meal, take some time to rest together, or have a contemplative conversation, give them a chance to come together as a group and appreciate how far they've come.

Atonement:

Though many of these sample scenes use a variety of story structures and genre conventions, I drew these next two directly from Joseph Campbell's Hero's Journey.

At its core, atonement is all about your protagonist recognizing their inner struggle for what it is and atoning for their earlier flaws. Here they can directly confront who they used to be and how much they've changed as a person. However, their character arc isn't over yet, so there should still be lingering flaws and struggles even after this scene.

Apotheosis:

Another scene drawn from the Hero's Journey, here your protagonist ascends to the status of a god. Of course, your version of this scene doesn't have to be quite so literal. Apotheosis is simply about your protagonist proving their character growth through action by showing their new skills and mindset at work.

Testing the Waters:

On the other hand, some protagonists may not be as bold as those who experience an Apotheosis scene. Others may need to test the waters first, gingerly trying out their new abilities and knowledge to see what they're capable of. Fortunately, this is a great chance for your protagonist to flex their muscles and gain a bit of confidence to help propel them forward from here on out.

True Power:

Your antagonist should also have a chance to show off their skills here.

This is in many ways a mirror of "The Antagonist's Power" scene from earlier in your story, and should act as a reminder that your conflict isn't over yet. The antagonist still has their own plans at work and the stakes are higher than ever. This is the perfect time to show off the true scope of their power, or at least strongly hint at it if you want to save that for the Climax.

Critical Knowledge:

Despite everything they learned at the Midpoint, your protagonist may still be seeking one final piece of the puzzle before they reach the Climax. This could be insight from a spiritual guide, an elder, or a mentor. Perhaps it's a special tool that will unlock the path to the final battle. Whatever it is, make sure they face significant challenges to get it and that it plays a meaningful role in the finale of your story.

A Boon:

Similarly, your protagonist may have a scene where they get to see how their new knowledge or skills can help others or heal their world. Unlike "Critical Knowledge," this scene will be more focused on how they can use these new tools, rather than on simply acquiring them. This is a great way to hint at the future Resolution of your story, even though your conflict isn't over quite yet.

The Road Back:

Depending on the story, your protagonist may need to journey back home in order to finally confront your antagonist. Perhaps they fled after being betrayed in Act 1 and are returning to reclaim their rightful place, or maybe they left to find a cure for a deadly disease and are finally returning to save their people.

Whatever their reason may be, it's possible you'll need to write a handful of scenes where your cast returns to where they started. Of course, don't forget that they've changed a lot since leaving home—they're bound to have some new thoughts and feelings about their old haunts when they return!

Consequences of the Journey:

As you get towards the end of Act 2.5, your protagonist will begin to see the cracks showing. We're approaching the darkest moment of their journey, so you may want to foreshadow that setback here.

This is a great time to reinforce the consequences your cast will face if your protagonist fails or, alternatively, the consequences of success. For instance, while failure may equal the death of those they hold dear, success may mean they can never return home again. The right choice is clear, but it's still important for them to wrestle with this choice.

Preparing for the Finale:

Before we reach the end of Act 2.5, your cast will need a final moment to prepare. They have a plan in place, but that plan likely requires certain traps to be set and tools gathered. This is their chance to get everything in order before they trigger the final battle of your story. Of course, not everything will work out as they expect, but we'll deal with that soon enough.

Betrayal:

At the very end of Act 2.5, your protagonist may experience a betrayal of some kind. This is all building towards the darkest moment of their journey and the beginning of Act 3, and could involve anything from a friend selling them out to a lover scorning them. Whether or not you include a scene like this (and how it ultimately plays out) will heavily depend on your personal story.

————

As I've said before, none of these scenes are a requirement—they're simply here to help inspire you.

Instead of feeling forced to include them, look at how they could fill out any gaps in your story or spark entirely new scenes. You could mix and match elements from multiple examples, ignore them all in favor of something else, or copy them verbatim. Whatever you choose, it's up to you and the unique needs of your story!

Hinting at What's to Come

I've been dropping the term "darkest moment" more and more often as we've gotten deeper into this challenge, because not everything is as rosy for your cast as it may seem.

Not only do they still need to face the final showdown with your antagonist, but they'll soon experience a major blow in the form of the Third Plot Point. To prepare for this setback, you'll want to hint at the cracks in your cast's armor early. This way, the sudden change in their circumstances won't feel unrealistic or contrived to your reader.

These hints will come in two forms: plot, and character.

As far as plot is concerned, you should begin foreshadowing the ways your antagonist will outsmart your cast's plans, whether through hidden traps or whatever other surprises they have in store. There's no need to reveal too much here, but you still want to leave a trail of breadcrumbs for your reader to follow. Let your cast fail in small ways or put them at risk to foreshadow your upcoming Third Plot Point.

Alongside these plot specific elements, you also need to keep your protagonist's character arc in mind.

At this point in your story, your protagonist is probably feeling pretty good about themselves—they may even believe they've solved their problems for good. However, we know better. Throughout the scenes leading up to your Third Plot Point, your reader should be able to see the remaining flaws in your protagonist and it should be apparent that their character arc isn't complete.

For instance, while Mulan gains the acceptance of her fellow soldiers after her Midpoint, she's still operating under a disguise. Most importantly, the movie makes sure we're always aware of how vulnerable she is, even as she scores more and more victories. She's almost discovered while bathing, and she's visibly uncomfortable when the men sing about their "ideal woman" and expect her to join in. All of this is building towards the moment they discover her true identity at the Third Plot Point.

Though subtle, these types of hints prime the audience and ensure readers feel compelled to continue reading. Make a point to reveal the cracks in your protagonist's armor in a similar way. After all, they still have a few demons to face, and their story would be much less interesting if they didn't!

A Reminder of the Stakes

While there are dozens if not hundreds of ways to highlight the weaknesses of your cast, raising the stakes is a pretty foolproof one. The stakes of your story should always be at the forefront of your readers' minds anyway, so it's easy for them to serve this dual purpose.

As your story inches closer to its Climax, you want the consequences of failure to be more and more apparent. Ask yourself:

- What will happen if your protagonist's plans fail?
- Who else might get caught in the crossfire of your story's conflict?
- How will your protagonist be affected by failure? What about the larger world?
- What does your protagonist still need to learn if they hope to succeed in the conflict?
- Which of your protagonist's personal goals might get in the way of this success?

After thinking through these questions, you should have a better idea of how the stakes of your conflict can manifest in your story. The goal here is to make it clear what the costs of failure will be, not only to your reader but to your cast itself. Fortunately, your writing doesn't need to be heavy-handed for this to work.

In *Princess Mononoke*, the story is blunt about the stakes of failure. If Ashitaka fails to stop the war between the humans and nature gods, destruction will ensue on a massive scale and the balance of nature will crumble. These are no small stakes, and the movie doesn't shy away from putting them front and center. However, for this story that makes sense —*Princess Mononoke* has a very clear moral message about humanity's role in nature, and these stakes reinforce that message. Meanwhile, they also put more emphasis on Ashitaka's own struggles to create peace between the two factions, effectively serving their dual purpose.

On the other hand, *Mulan* shows off its stakes more subtly.

While much of this phase of Mulan's journey focuses on how uncomfortable she is hiding her true identity, the movie also shows us the carnage and destruction the Huns are causing. Death is a constant reality for these characters, doubly so if they fail. The movie even calls attention to the abandoned doll of a young girl, presumably killed in the fighting— specifically highlighting the extra vulnerability of women, like Mulan. It's not as blatant as Ashitaka's stakes, but it still showcases the danger Mulan is in, both from her enemies and from her supposed allies. After all, earlier in the movie the audience watched as her father warned her family that, if she's discovered, she'll be killed for treason.

Ultimately, no matter how you highlight the stakes of your story, try to find ways that serve a dual purpose.

Do these stakes relate to your character's inner journey, and how could they foreshadow the struggles they've yet to face? Perhaps your stakes apply mainly to your story's plot. Either way, keep these in mind as you write and weave them into your story organically whenever you can. This way, the final confrontation with your antagonist and the setback your protagonist must face beforehand will feel like they've been building in the background this whole time.

The Goals of Day Seven

With Day Seven at its end, don't worry—you haven't gone back in time to Day Four, and I promise there are only three days left in this challenge!

Though a lot of what you worked on today may feel similar to what you've written before, I hope you still found something fresh and exciting in today's scenes. Soon, all the plot threads, characters, subplots, and themes you've been weaving into your story will come to fruition.

It's an exciting time, even if it does trigger a bit of deja vu.

Tomorrow we'll weather the final blow before the finale of your story, but for now, here are the goals you've completed for Day Seven:

1. Brainstorm a new series of goals for your cast, this time building towards your Climax.
2. Foreshadow the Third Plot Point, which we'll begin writing tomorrow.
3. Highlight the stakes of your story's conflict as a reminder for both your reader and protagonist.
4. Specifically hint at the inner struggle your

protagonist still needs to face before completing
their character arc.

By the end of today, your draft should have approximately
twenty eight completed scenes (or thirty five thousand
words) and you should be approaching the Third Plot Point
of your story.

On to Day Eight!

9

DAY EIGHT: APPROACHING THE END

"Things always get worse before they get better."

As clichéd as this statement may be, it holds a lot of truth. How many times have you felt stressed to the point of exhaustion, overwhelmed by work, family, or friends, only for the wave to break over your head? It probably felt like things could never improve, but as the surf rolled past, you stood up again.

You finally completed the project hanging over your head at work, and now you look back on it with pride. The tension between you and your dear friend taught you why you valued them in the first place, and now your relationship has flourished. Whatever your experience was, these difficult moments are often where we learn the most about ourselves, helping us grow into much stronger, happier people in the long run.

Today, your protagonist will have to face their own darkest moment, before hopefully standing up when it's all over. This will be the final test of their inner journey, and you'll need to pull out all the stops to make them truly question who they are, what they want, and why they set out on this journey to begin with. These next few scenes will be difficult, but by the end your protagonist will have stepped over the threshold as a newly formed character, ready to face the coming Climax.

Of course, you may be feeling a bit of darkness too.

We're reaching the end of this challenge, and the last seven days have no doubt started to wear on you. You're deep enough into the challenge to feel exhausted, but not close enough to the finish line to see the light on the other side. Ironically, as I sit here writing this, I'm feeling the same way about this book. It has been a marathon few months of testing, writing, and editing to bring this guide to life, and though I'm ready to call it finished, I recognize it's not quite there yet.

By the time you're reading this, I know I'll be holding this book in my hands, confident that the work was worth it. However, right now that light is hard to see. I have no doubt you're feeling the same way about your novel, but trust me— you only have three days left, and soon you and I both will be looking back on our work with pride.

Today, you'll just need to focus on propelling your story through this dark and stormy night.

The Third Plot Point

If you remember our discussion of story structure from way back on Day Three, then you should remember the Third Plot Point—this is the darkness your protagonist is about to face, and it marks your story's shift into Act 3.

Here's how we defined the Third Plot Point:

- **The Third Plot Point:** This plot point marks the end of Act 2 and is a harsh reality check for your protagonist. Here they'll suffer a major defeat at the hands of your antagonist, throwing their previous plans into disarray. This will be their lowest moment, when they feel like they've lost everything. In the following scenes, they'll need to reassess their goals in order to recommit to the journey ahead.

As you can see, this plot point serves two distinct roles. Not only does it challenge your protagonist emotionally and mentally, but it throws a final twist into the plot of your novel. This twist is, at its core, all about raising the stakes of your story one final time.

You see, during your Third Plot Point, whatever plans your characters had in place will be ruined, or at least significantly altered. Perhaps the weakness they thought the antagonist had turns out to be a red herring, or maybe the antagonist had been preparing for their plans all along. Maybe a secret they've been keeping is discovered, or the knowledge they gained at the Midpoint turns out to be a lie. Often, the Third Plot Point will also isolate your protagonist, not only ruining their plans but robbing them of the support of their allies—at least temporarily. This is yet another way to test them, adding one more layer of mental strain for them to overcome.

No matter how you throw your protagonist's life into disarray, you should strike directly at the heart of their plans and their mind. Think carefully about how you can up the ante and change the rules of the game in a way that's new and frightening.

Of course, this scene of your story is not only about raising the stakes and increasing the tension, but about forcing your protagonist to *earn* their victory. This dark moment forces them to make a choice: either surrender and lose the fight, or rise up in the face of this final test.

They'll still have to face the Climax in the coming scenes, but they'll never even reach this Climax if they can't surpass this final challenge.

Testing the Mind

While your Climax will be the most challenging moment of your plot, the Third Plot Point should be the most challenging moment for your protagonist's mind.

Throughout your story they've been reaching towards a clear goal until, suddenly, the Third Plot Point snatches that away. To make matters worse, it does so by playing on all of their weaknesses, fears, flaws, and vulnerabilities. While they likely thought they had solved their problems after the Midpoint, the Third Plot Point will prove that they haven't, and you can see this at work in all the stories below:

- *Mulan*: Mulan's fellow soldiers discover her gender, and she avoids execution only because she saved her commander's life. Her friends abandon her in the mountains, alone, unwanted, and disgraced—all because of who she truly is.
- *How to Train Your Dragon*: Hiccup's father captures Toothless and forces him to lead the Vikings to the Dragon's Nest. Not only does he ignore Hiccup's warnings, but he disowns Hiccup and labels him a traitor. Hiccup is now truly alone, having lost not

only his best friend, but any hope he might have had of one day being accepted as a Viking.

- *Star Wars: A New Hope*: While trapped inside the Death Star, Obi-Wan sacrifices himself to help Luke and his friends escape, and Luke is left to watch as Darth Vader kills Obi-Wan. Obi-Wan's ghost urges him to flee, and Luke and his friends narrowly escape Darth Vader's clutches.
- *Princess Mononoke*: Ashitaka finally reaches the Deer God, wounded and near death. However, though the Deer God heals his physical wounds, Ashitaka wakes up to find his curse remains. Despite journeying far from home and sacrificing so much to seek the Deer God's help, it has rejected his pleas.

Not only have these characters' plans taken a hit, but they've realized that their inner struggle isn't over. The strength and knowledge they've gained still isn't enough to overcome the conflict, and they're left to pick up the pieces.

As you can see, this is a difficult, painful time for your protagonist. Don't shy away from bringing all of their fears and vulnerabilities into play as you test their mental strength. The Third Plot Point is a time of darkness, and it's why your cast's journey was still far from over after the Midpoint.

A Different Kind of Energy

There's no doubt your cast is in a dark place at this point in your story and, as we discussed earlier, you're probably feeling a bit of darkness as well. Normally I'd encourage you to remain light-hearted and enjoy everything you can about bringing your story to life—however, this scene requires a different approach.

The Third Plot Point is a painful, melancholy, and even aggressive scene, making it the perfect time to lean into any negative feelings or self-doubt this challenge has brought on. Channel your frustration and tiredness into harsh, sharp prose. Don't be afraid to beat your characters down. Once you've ruined their plans, let yourself sit with the emotional turmoil your protagonist is experiencing. Much like the aftermath of the Midpoint, this is a good time to explore deep into your protagonist's mindset. Give them the time to reflect on the journey they've faced and the failures they've just experienced.

Of course, channeling this frustration isn't easy for everyone. You may be a genuinely cheery person, someone who rarely indulges in more aggressive emotions. On the other hand, perhaps you simply don't know how to express these feelings in words.

That's ok.

Remember that your first draft is about getting your story down on paper, not perfecting your prose. If you don't know how to write about the complex emotions your protagonist is feeling, simply state that they're angry/sad/afraid/hurt/et cetera. While these cut-and-dry descriptions aren't ideal for a final novel, you'll have plenty of time to infuse more action and emotion into these scenes when you sit down to edit your draft later on.

To keep yourself motivated today in the midst of all this negative energy, you should also try mixing things up. Write in a new location, or write alongside friends. Play music that captures the dark tone of the Third Plot Point, or contrast the tension of what you're writing with something cheery and light.

Above all, don't be afraid to make this scene intense.

While it should still fit with the overall tone of your novel and genre, this emotional intensity is what the Third Plot Point is all about. There's rarely a reason to shy away from it.

The Time to Recover

Of course, in the aftermath of the Third Plot Point, your protagonist needs a reason to hope.

While the Third Plot Point is undoubtedly dark and painful, it's more about hope than anything else. Like the cliché goes, things get worse before they get better, and that will (hopefully) be true for your protagonist here.

Despite this stumbling block, they've grown a lot throughout their journey. They've learned new skills and gained new allies, and they're likely stronger than they think. However, they probably don't see that right now, especially after the massive setback of the Third Plot Point.

This is why your protagonist needs a moment to rest and reflect on everything that's happened to them. Give them a chance to relive their journey thus far, and help them draw on these experiences to find the strength to continue forward. Most importantly, force them to finally confront their inner struggle head on.

Mulan spends her entire journey hiding who she truly is in order to gain others' approval. After her Midpoint, she convinces herself this disguise is ok, that she can pull it off while still achieving her goals.

However, Mulan's Third Plot Point snatches that disguise away and exposes her to the world, and this is her story's way of demanding that she learns to value herself. While it's not easy, in the aftermath of her darkest moment she realizes her dedication to her friends and her country is more important than her gender. It's this realization that gives her the strength to stand back up in the face of her society's scorn and continue on.

Likewise, Hiccup has been trying to conform to his father's expectations his entire life—and consistently failing to do so. Slowly but surely, his journey has proven to him that his unique skills are worthwhile, but he continued to hide behind the facade of a "good Viking" out of a fear of the truth. Finally, hoping his friendship with Toothless will convince his father that dragons aren't evil, he reveals what he's learned only to be struck down.

Not only does he lose Toothless, but he's disowned by the Vikings. Everything he wanted disappears, and he's left alone to pick up the pieces. Yet, he knows he was right. Dragons *aren't* evil, and this belief in his discovery gives him the strength he needs to defy his father and eventually save his best friend.

As you can see, the goal here isn't to beat your protagonist down permanently, but to back them into a corner where the only way out is by embracing their truth. So, give them a glimmer of hope and then let them stand up stronger in the face of everything they've experienced.

From there, it's simply a matter of regrouping, creating a new plan, and marching towards the Climax.

The Goals of Day Eight

Despite the stress of this challenge and of today's goals, I hope you feel proud of all that you've accomplished. Just like your protagonist must face some difficult times before they can emerge on the other side, you've no doubt had your fair share of bad days.

Still, you've completed Day Eight, meaning you only have two days left in this challenge. Next up we'll get into the Climax of your story and the conclusion of this epic journey, but for now I hope you'll take some time to rest. Our adventure together isn't quite over, but we're nearly there!

Tomorrow we'll face the finale of your story, but for now, here are the goals you've completed for Day Eight:

1. Throw your protagonist's plans into disarray, specifically highlighting their flaws in the process.
2. Show the aftermath of your protagonist's failure and make them question their journey thus far.
3. Give your protagonist a glimmer of hope and help them finally overcome their inner struggle.
4. Guide your cast as they regroup and march forward towards the Climax.

By the end of today, your draft should have approximately thirty two completed scenes (or forty thousand words) and your story's Third Plot Point should be complete.

On to Day Nine!

10

DAY NINE: THE FINAL FIGHT

W hen you watch your favorite movie or read a beloved book, the Climax is the moment you live for. Everything in that story has been winding its way to this final moment, building towards something powerful and compelling, and you'll no doubt think about what occurs here for weeks to come.

This sense of excitement is doubled for authors.

You see, for many authors this is the part of their story that inspired them in the first place. Months or years ago they imaged a character facing incredible odds in a powerful final battle, or brainstormed a couple coming together after months of strife. Whatever your novel's Climax is, this is where your story finally pays off for both you and your readers.

Of course, you're probably not ready to write your story's Climax quite yet. You may be standing in the doorway, but today is just as much about crossing that threshold as it is about writing a stellar Climax itself. From getting your cast into position, to choosing your protagonist's final outcome, there are a lot of big decisions to make today. However, don't worry—everything you've been creating has prepared you for this moment.

Today, all you have to do is bring those things to fruition!

Remembering Your Spark

Much like yesterday, today you'll want to take a moment before you begin writing to consider your upcoming scenes.

Just like the Third Plot Point, the Climax is an emotionally intense part of your story and your cast will be under a lot of stress as a result. You'll want to capture these feelings as much as possible. Fortunately, taking a moment to consider your cast's mindset can go a long way towards making today's writing flow more easily.

It's also likely that the Climax is one of those scenes you've been daydreaming about for a while. Personally, the Climax is often the first thing I think of when creating a new story, and it's this spark of inspiration that drives me to continue writing until I complete my draft. Many other writers I've talked to describe a similar experience.

Of course, even if this isn't the case for you, your Climax is what you've been building towards for eight days. You should have a strong idea of what needs to happen here as a result. How will your characters begin the final fight? How will they try to succeed, and how will your antagonist counter their plans?

All of these questions should be easy to answer with a bit of brainstorming, even if you're unsure of them at first glance.

Before you begin writing today, give yourself a solid fifteen or twenty minutes to imagine this final phase of your story. Let these scenes play out in your head, and jot down a few brief notes about what you see. These will guide you as you write your Climax.

Of course, you'll also have some more practical decisions to make today:

- Where will your Climax take place?
- Who will be present, and why?
- What tone will your Climax have?
- What do you want your readers to take away from these scenes?

This is one final time where your collection will come in extremely handy. Don't be afraid to take a moment to flip through the images, music clips, and quotes you've collected to get yourself in the right frame of mind to write your Climax. Your collection can also help inspire you as you describe the various set pieces of your finale, so it should definitely be a part of any brainstorming you do today.

In the end, the best thing you can do for yourself and your writing is to enjoy the process. You're steps away from the finish line, and the energy and excitement of these final scenes should help carry you through today's goals—let yourself relish in the action and have fun!

Don't Delay

At the start of today's writing session, it's entirely possible you won't be ready to begin your Climax just yet. While you should have finished your Third Plot Point yesterday, you may still be dealing with the aftermath of that scene.

If that's the case, then you have some housekeeping to do.

For starters, make sure your protagonist gets the time they need to process the events of the Third Plot Point. This period of reflection is extremely important to their story—it'll not only help them recommit to the fight ahead, but it'll force them to fully embrace the main lesson of their character arc.

Once this period of reflection is taken care of, you can shift your focus fully towards the Climax.

Your main task here is to get your characters in position for their final fight. However, be careful not to let your story meander aimlessly at this stage. You've officially entered Act 3 and, unlike the two halves of Act 2, this act should be laser focused on bringing your story to its conclusion.

- **Act 3 (Resolution):** Act 3 is the final quarter of your novel and sees the conflict come to its end. Here your protagonist and antagonist will have their final confrontation. Once you resolve the conflict of your story, you'll have a moment to hint at the future and explain what happens after your protagonist's journey is over (or set up a sequel, if you're planning one).

This means every scene after the Third Plot Point and leading into your Climax should focus on one thing and one thing alone: setting up the final confrontation of your story. This is where you'll resolve any outstanding subplots or character arcs—specifically ones your Climax won't resolve itself—and you should also ensure your cast is where they need to be before the Climax starts. Any plans that need to be laid or traps that need to be set should be done here as well. Once the pieces are in place, your Climax can begin without delay.

Of course, you may wonder why this urgency is necessary. At the end of the day, this is really a favor to your reader. Part of why we've been focusing so much on story structure throughout this challenge is because it creates a steady sense of rising tension for your reader, encouraging them to stay invested in your protagonist's adventure.

In this final phase of your story, your reader has just watched your protagonist get kicked to the ground in every sense of the word. Now they've watched them stand back up again. For a reader, this "strength against all odds" is intoxicating. They're ready for the final fight and are rooting for your protagonist more than they ever will be. Unfortunately, nothing diminishes that excitement more than an extended series of meandering scenes—if you want to capitalize on your reader's enthusiasm, you need to do so now.

Writing the Climax

With everyone in their places, you can finally begin the finale of your story. Like we discussed back on Day Three, the Climax of your novel will serve a crucial role:

- **The Climax:** This is the final conflict between your protagonist and antagonist. It may be a major battle, a confession of love, or a heated confrontation. Whatever it is, your protagonist will need to draw on all the skills, knowledge, and alliances they've gained throughout your story if they want to succeed. Alternatively, they may fail if they're a negative arc character.

Unlike most of the other plot points you've written so far, your Climax can actually consist of a handful of scenes, rather than just one. This is especially true since it's such an involved part of your story. Still, just like the lead up to the Climax, the Climax itself shouldn't drag on unnecessarily. You'll want to maintain the forward momentum your readers are feeling, so every scene in your Climax should reveal something new and intense that directly impacts the conclusion of your story.

For instance, the Climax of Mulan takes around two scenes from start to finish. As soon as the Huns reveal themselves and capture the Emperor, the Climax begins, and Mulan sets out to enlist her fellow soldiers' help. Then we transition into a new scene as Mulan and her allies enter the Emperor's palace and engage the Huns. The Climax finally ends when the Emperor escapes and Mulan uses her cleverness to defeat the Huns' leader.

As you can see, the focus here (and in your own Climax) should be on the conflict of your story above all else. Whatever that conflict is, this is where everything comes to a head.

Of course, the type of conflict you're dealing with will largely depend on your unique story. In a coming-of-age movie like Mulan, the conflict is highly plot-driven. On the other hand, a romance novel may have a more character-centric conflict.

Still, as a general rule your story's plot will be your focus during the Climax. While your cast will get a chance to show off their growth as characters, none of this can happen without the plot being resolved in the process. Don't lose the forest for the trees here. You'll get a final few moments to bring closure to your characters' arcs after the Climax, but your plot needs to reach its conclusion before any of that can happen.

Of course, if at any point you find yourself wondering how your story's conflict should end, think back to the question your story has been asking since the beginning.

Will the lovers finally reunite? Will unicorns return to Earth? Will the Vikings defeat the dragon hoard? Whatever you've encouraged your readers to wonder throughout your story should be what you answer during your Climax.

Speaking of Vikings and dragons, let's look at the Climax of *How to Train your Dragon.*

This movie's climax begins when Hiccup and the other kids arrive at the Dragon's Nest. Hiccup's father has led the Vikings to the nest in hopes of destroying it, using the captive Toothless as a guide. However, they quickly realize that the mother dragon, the Red Death, is far more powerful than they can handle.

Fortunately, Hiccup and the others arrive just in time to distract the Red Death, and Hiccup jumps into the fray to find Toothless. In the process, his father helps him free Toothless and admits he was wrong about the dragons and about Hiccup. Finally getting the approval he had always craved, Hiccup returns to battle alongside Toothless, luring the Red Death into the clouds. After an intense fight, the pair defeats the Red Death, but Toothless' prosthetic tail fin burns up in the process. He and Hiccup crash to the ground and the Climax ends with Toothless revealing an alive but wounded Hiccup cradled in his wings.

As you can see, the story wastes no time here. Not only that, but every major character plays an important role. The other kids Hiccup has been competing with throughout his story come to help him, and he and his father get a moment of reconciliation. Likewise, your Climax should involve all the major players from your cast in some way, so long as it makes sense in the context of your novel.

Of course, above and beyond your other cast members, your protagonist has a unique role to play here.

Remember the First Plot Point? Your protagonist made a choice there that propelled them into the conflict of your story, and they should make an equally powerful choice to resolve that conflict. This is why they need to remain an active player until the very end of the Climax, ultimately determining the outcome of your novel. Don't hesitate to showcase everything they've learned and gained throughout their journey. What's more, let your antagonist truly test their skills—after all, they need to earn their victory.

Can they really uphold the lessons they've learned? Will they stay strong in the face of this final challenge?

The Outcome of Your Story

Of course, both of these questions raise an even bigger one: how will your story end?

You see, not all protagonists' stories end the same way. Back on Day Two we talked about the different character arcs your protagonist could follow, and while I haven't pushed you to worry about these too much thus far, all three will come back into play here.

As a refresher, here are the three types of character arcs your protagonist might fall under:

Positive Arc:

This is the classic "hero" story, though it can apply equally to many types of characters.

In a positive arc, the character starts out with a deep internal flaw. Throughout the course of their arc the story's conflict punishes this flaw. They face a major challenge that leads to a turning point in their arc, moving them closer to uncovering the lesson they need to learn. Ultimately—despite setbacks along the way—they learn to embrace this new truth, overcome their flaws, and succeed against the conflict of their story.

- **Examples:** Rick Blaine, Harry Potter, Aragorn, Han Solo, Hiccup

Negative Arc:

Negative arcs follow a similar trajectory as positive arcs, with the major change being at the end.

Just like a positive arc, the character begins the story with an internal flaw and—as the story progresses—uncovers an important truth, experiencing a key turning point along the way. However, unlike a positive arc, a negative arc character rejects that truth repeatedly. By the end of the story they're more entrenched in their flaws than before, growing into a worse version of themselves and failing against the conflict of their story as a result.

- **Examples:** Anakin Skywalker, Jay Gatsby, Michael Corleone, Tyler Durden, Sansa Stark

Flat Arc:

These are the black sheep of character arcs.

While positive and negative arcs are "change arcs," a flat arc character already knows their truth at the start of the story. Instead, their arc is about upholding their truth in the face of their story's conflict, passing their lesson to others in the process.

- **Examples:** Captain America, Katniss Everdeen, Luke Skywalker, Princess Nausicaä, Mattie Ross

———

As you can tell from these definitions, positive and flat arcs end similarly. These are the traditional characters you think of when someone mentions a hero, and this pantheon includes both positive arc characters like Mulan and flat arc ones like Ashitaka. At the end of a positive character arc the character succeeds, resolving the conflict of their story while simultaneously completing the journey of personal growth they've been following.

Negative arcs, however, follow a slightly different path—and the Climax is where these differences really begin to show.

A negative arc character has been facing all the same challenges as their positive counterparts, but where Luke Skywalker learned the right lessons, Anakin learned the wrong ones. Whenever Luke faced a new hurdle, he leaned harder into the Force, worked harder to show mercy and respect, and fought harder for what he believed was just. At the end of his trilogy, he rejected the Dark Side and defeated the Emperor as a result.

Anakin, on the other hand, wasn't so lucky.

As a negative arc character, Anakin's fear of loss slowly ate away at him over the course of his story. His fear of leaving behind his mother and of losing Padme, though justified by past experiences, morphed into a desperate obsession with control. Instead of learning to trust and heal after these traumatic experiences, Anakin learned to crave power above all else. This need for control was his primary flaw, and if he was a positive arc character he would have found ways to overcome it. However, as a negative arc character this flaw consumes Anakin, until he ends his trilogy as the villain Luke will have to decades years later.

While every character will have their own nuances and specific patterns, this cuts a pretty clear contrast between the journeys of positive and negative arc characters.

Even though negative arc characters may succeed in some parts of their story, they're fighting a losing battle against their own inner demons. The Climax is where this path will finally split from the positive arc for good, meaning this is where you'll have to decide which road your protagonist will follow: positive, flat, or negative?

If positive or flat, they'll likely succeed here, overcoming their flaw and the conflict all at once. If negative, they'll fail on both counts. Even if they do somehow succeed against the conflict, they'll have used the wrong methods to get there, and victory will feel hollow.

Of course, by this point in your story you may or may not have laid the groundwork needed to convincingly sell a negative (or even positive) character arc. We didn't focus on this topic for a reason, because you'll have plenty of time—

along with a more robust understanding of your story—to edit these elements after you finish your first draft. For now, simply decide how your protagonist's story will end and bring that ending to fruition here.

The Goals of Day Nine

With your Climax complete, you've officially wrapped up the conflict of your story. I hope you gave yourself license to sink your teeth into the action and excitement of this pivotal scene. After all, tomorrow will bring the final day of this challenge *and* the final moments of your story—and things will likely get a little bittersweet.

Either way, whether you relished in writing your Climax or are just excited to be on the home stretch, this challenge is almost at its end. There's little left to do beyond wrapping up the last threads of your story and saying goodbye to your cast, but that's a task for tomorrow.

For today, I'd say you've won some hard earned rest!

Tomorrow we'll complete your first draft at last, but for now, here are the goals you've completed for Day Nine:

1. Visualize your Climax, taking notes on any important elements.
2. Finalize any of your cast's preparations before triggering the final confrontation of your story.
3. Begin your story's Climax, paying special attention to how your protagonist will resolve the conflict.
4. Decide on your protagonist's final outcome— positive, flat, or negative—and use that to write the final moments of your Climax.

By the end of today, your draft should have approximately thirty six completed scenes (or forty five thousand words) and the Climax of your story should be complete.

On to Day Ten!

11

DAY TEN: DAWN OF THE LAST DAY

These days, the simple phrase "The End" closes so many stories that it has become something of a cliché—and to the outsider, it no doubt seems like lazy writing.

However, when you think about the author behind those words and the strange emotions they must be feeling, it's easier to see why this short statement of fact feels fitting. Everything they've been working towards is at its end, and while it's both a relief and a joy to finish a novel, it's also bittersweet.

For me personally, the feeling of completing any book is a strange one. On the one hand it's exhilarating, but on the other I simply feel exhausted. By the end of a book I'm always ready for a long nap—and I imagine you are too—but I can never sleep. Instead, I sit quietly looking at my draft for a while, before finally turning off my laptop, stretching my legs, and going for a walk.

It feels good to be back in the world after so many days away.

Your Final Farewell

When you sit down to write today, you'll no doubt be feeling a lot. These final scenes of your novel are your chance to say goodbye, not only to your cast but to your story's unique world and history.

Most of all, it's your chance to say farewell to this challenge.

So, while it can be tempting to pause and read back over everything you've written so far, resist the urge. The time to edit and review your work will come soon, but for now your challenge isn't quite over!

Instead, take this time before you begin writing to consider what you loved most about this story and everything you've created. Channel that pride into these final few scenes, highlighting whatever you loved most about this crazy adventure. While there are some plot related things to take care of today, in reality Day Ten is all about you and your story spending your final moments together.

Their Mark on This World

In terms of the last, plot-related elements we need to wrap up today, there are only a few.

For starters, this portion of your story is the (aptly named) Resolution, and as it might sound this final phase of your novel is all about showing the aftermath of the Climax.

- **The Resolution:** These are the last few scenes of your story, meant to show your readers the final effects of your Climax. Whether your protagonist succeeded or failed in their quest, here you'll take a moment to say some final goodbyes and show what your story's world will look like going forward. You may also lay the groundwork for sequels here.

When you write your Resolution today, you'll want to start by considering the consequences of your story's conflict. This is your chance to showcase not only why your story mattered for your cast, but why it mattered for the world around them as well.

For instance, Mulan's journey not only healed her relationship with her family, but saved China from invasion. Hiccup not only gained his father's pride, but brought peace to the Vikings and their new dragon companions. Luke learned the ways of the Force and took down the brutal Empire in the process. Finally, Ashitaka lifted his curse while helping humans and nature live alongside one another. All of these characters had a deep impact, not only on themselves and the people closest to them, but on their societies. Good or bad, subtle or not, your protagonist will leave a mark on their world as well.

So, think about the effects of their journey. What does their victory (or defeat) mean for their world, allies, enemies, and friends? How can you show these effects in action through your Resolution?

Of course, as with the rest of Act 3, you don't want to linger here.

Just like the Climax, your Resolution can take up multiple scenes, and probably will. However, you shouldn't let your story wander. The Resolution is at its best when it's short and sweet, delivering your final message while your reader is still energized and emotional from the Climax of your story.

Your goal here is to present a final picture of what your characters' lives will be like after readers close the last page of your novel, possibly hinting at any sequels coming down the road. How does life go on for your characters? How will their lives be different after the journey they've just completed? What final lesson do you want your readers to take away from your story?

Often, characters will return home at this point, finally finding peace. Others can never return home, too changed to fit back into the daily hum-drum of life.

Whatever the case is for your protagonist, this is the chance to provide a parting glimpse into the world they've created.

Ways to End Your Story

Just like there are many ways to start a story, there are just as many ways to end it. If you're at a loss for how best to bring this adventure to a close, here are some common methods that might suit your story.

———

The Chronological Ending:

Perhaps one of the easiest Resolutions to write is the chronological one.

This ending comes directly after the Climax, showing your characters wrapping up the final fight and moving on with their lives. They might gather together and discuss their plans for the future, or they may simply go their separate ways. Often, characters will travel onward to their next adventure, either as a group or alone.

A Return to the Normal World:

In these endings, your cast will travel home after the fight is over—think of stories like *Alice in Wonderland* or *The Chronicles of Narnia*. This gives your characters the chance to return to where they started, though they've changed in fundamental and often transformative ways. As a result, they'll see their normal world in a new light, and will likely be more at peace as a result.

Alternatively, they may be so deeply changed that they can never quite return to a normal life, forcing them to journey onward in search of something more.

Striking a Contrast:

While you can incorporate this specific ending into many of the others, it's too important not to mention on its own. Here, your protagonist will face a situation similar to one they faced at the start of their journey. However, instead of falling back into old habits they'll stop and reflect on everything they've learned, and this time they'll choose a different option.

Perhaps they were cruel to a character early on, but this time show kindness, or maybe something they were once afraid of no longer frightens them. Whatever it may be, this ending is a great way to highlight the growth your character has undergone, simply by showing how their actions have changed.

A Jump Forward:

The Jump Forward ending sees your story jump forward in time to a period anywhere from years to decades after the events of your main story. Members of your cast, now older, reminisce about their experiences on their journey—this is often done for a younger audience, as a way of preserving their adventure. Instead of directly narrating their story, they may also write a memoir or record their experiences in some other way.

This ending has the benefit of providing hindsight and context to your characters' experiences, since they've now had years to process what they went through.

The Storyteller:

Finally, this ending is told by a character that was never part of the main story to begin with, meaning this can play out a few different ways. In some instances, this character is a literal storyteller that exists within the world of your novel, relaying the events to others also in their world like the puppeteer in *The Hunchback of Notre Dame*. Alternatively, they may be a narrator who tells the story in the real world, such as the grandfather in *The Princess Bride*.

While you can theoretically use this Resolution in any story, it's best if you set it up as a framing device early on. If you choose this ending, consider tweaking the opening of your story during editing to introduce this outside narrator from the beginning.

———

Of course, there are dozens of ways to wrap up your novel—these are just some of the most common.

Whether you use one of these verbatim or mix and match elements from all of them, just remember that your Resolution is a final glimpse into your story's world. This is your chance to provide a parting message that ties your whole novel together, so pick an ending that matches the needs of your personal story.

Some Final Thoughts on this Challenge

As our time together comes to a close, I want to address one final thing. You see, at its core this challenge was meant as exactly that: a challenge.

When you sit down to write your second, third, or even fourth novel, I doubt you'll follow this process again. In many ways, this was never meant to be more than a one-time challenge, and I honestly think that's a good thing. The last ten days have been intense, filled with hard work and many compromises, but all of it was in service of a single goal— proving that, *yes*, you can write a novel.

So many dreamers never become writers because they don't think they're good enough, and far too many writers never become authors because they believe writing a novel is just too hard. They make up roadblocks in their head, never realizing that, in reality, they just need to sit down and write.

Yes, writing a novel is hard, and *yes*, it's not as easy as just sitting down and putting words on a page. However, it's also not much harder than that—and now you know what it really takes.

With this challenge at its end, you've broken down the mental barriers that told you you weren't capable of writing a novel—and guess what? Clearly they were wrong! What's more, now you have the experience needed to repeat this success for as many stories as you want to tell.

When you sit down to write your second novel, you'll have your own system to follow and your own habits to fall back on. Slowly but surely writing can become a more sustainable part of your life, something you do a small amount of every day rather than all at once. Yet, in the background, these ten days will always serve as a reminder that writing a novel isn't impossible—that, in fact, nothing is ever impossible—and that you've done it before.

While your writing journey is far from over, you've crossed perhaps the biggest hurdle on your quest to become an author. Your story is complete and alive on the page, ready for you to polish into something amazing. Tomorrow it'll be time for editing, but for tonight, I think it's time to celebrate.

What do you think?

Your new to-do list:

- Go for a long run with your dog.
- Invite friends over and talk about nothing book related for hours.
- Cook a delicious meal to share with those you love.
- Curl up with a beloved book.
- Binge watch TV for a few hours.
- Eat ice cream with a serving spoon.
- Frolic in the fields.
- Be proud!

Tonight you're officially holding the first draft of your novel in your hands. Here are the goals you've completed for Day Ten:

1. Decide how to spend your story's final moments.

2. Show the consequences of your story's Climax and hint at how your cast's lives might go on from here.
3. Say one last goodbye to your story's world and characters.
4. Celebrate! You've earned it.

By the end of today, your draft should be complete at approximately forty scenes (or fifty thousand words).

WHAT COMES NEXT?

As you close the back cover of this book, I want you to know —you've done an amazing thing!

Writing the first draft of a novel is no easy task. However, it's also not an *impossible* task, and you've proved that you have what it takes. I'm so happy to see you reach this point and I hope you're proud of the draft you've created, regardless of its flaws.

Next you'll need to edit your draft, but trust me when I say the hardest part is over. You have a strong foundation to work from, meaning all that's left is to polish the rough edges and turn your manuscript into a finished novel.

Of course, if you have any questions (or just want to brag about your upcoming book launch) send me an email through my website!

When I'm not busy writing books like these and getting lost in my own fictional worlds, I run **The Novel Smithy**, a site dedicated to giving new writers the tools they need to create their dream novels.

Finally, if you enjoyed this book, leaving a review would not only help me, but other writers as well. Reviews are how readers like you find the books they're looking for, so I hope you'll take a moment to leave some honest feedback.

With that said, this book—and your novel writing challenge —is officially complete!

Happy Writing,

Lewis Jorstad

ABOUT THE AUTHOR

Lewis Jorstad is a writer, author, and book coach, a lover of reading and travel, and a child at heart living in central Virginia. He hopes to visit every country in the world before he dies, but for now he spends his time teaching up-and-coming writers the skills they need to create compelling, successful novels.

You can find more of his work over at **The Novel Smithy:**

https://thenovelsmithy.com/

Before you go...

Are you struggling to keep track of your story?

If you're ready to get your ideas organized, download your
FREE copy of my Story Bible Template.

It's the perfect companion to this series, and the perfect tool
for creating a clear, bird's-eye view of your novel!

https://thenovelsmithy.com/story-template/

THE COMPLETE TEN DAY DRAFTING PROCESS

If you ever need a reminder of the goals you've completed throughout this challenge, here they are in an easy to reference format:

———

Day Zero: How to Write a Novel

1. Find a space that nurtures your creativity and set it up with any necessary supplies.
2. Mark ten writing days and two mercy days on your calendar, keeping in mind any major commitments that might delay your progress.
3. If you don't have one already, create a brief outline that covers your story's plot, characters, worldbuilding, conflict, and (optionally) your scenes.
4. Based on the number of scenes in your outline, set goals for yourself and add them to your calendar.

Day One: Finding the Right Mindset

1. Master your mindset and embrace the idea of an imperfect first draft.
2. Choose a tense and point of view for your novel and write them either in your outline or at the top of your draft.
3. Hook your readers with the opening scene of your story.
4. Introduce your protagonist, along with any basic information about your story's world, settings, and characters.

Day Two: Developing a Routine

1. Establish a healthy writing routine that discourages you from listening to your inner editor.
2. Introduce the main conflict of your novel to both your protagonist and reader.
3. Find what motivates your protagonist using their character arc, want, and need.
4. Start showing why your protagonist needs to get involved in the main conflict.

Day Three: The Journey Begins

1. Mark any changes you've made to your story in your outline—consider making this a regular practice going forward.
2. Create a page in your outline for questions or topics you want to research later.
3. Write your story's First Plot Point, ensuring your protagonist makes an active choice to begin their journey.
4. Show off the immediate consequences of your protagonist's decision.

Day Four: The Trials of Act 2

1. Create a collection of inspiration for whenever you need a boost of inspiration.
2. List the goals of your cast leading into the Midpoint and use these as a reference while writing.
3. Challenge your characters in meaningful ways, specifically focusing on how these challenges push them to confront their inner struggles.
4. If needed, incorporate common scene types into your story to keep your plot moving forward.

Day Five: Halfway Day

1. Write your story's Midpoint, paying special attention to how it shifts your cast from reaction to action.

Day Six: Fighting Burnout

1. Create a plan to address burnout, and then put that plan into action.
2. Consider the new skills and knowledge your cast has gained and how these will contribute to some well-earned victories.
3. Bring your cast together to reassess their goals and formulate a new plan of action.
4. Remember: while this second phase of your novel may feel a lot like the first, there are fundamental differences to keep in mind.

Day Seven: Writer's Deja Vu

1. Brainstorm a new series of goals for your cast, this time building towards your Climax.

2. Foreshadow the Third Plot Point, which we'll begin writing tomorrow.
3. Highlight the stakes of your story's conflict as a reminder for both your reader and protagonist.
4. Specifically hint at the inner struggle your protagonist still needs to face before completing their character arc.

Day Eight: Approaching the End

1. Throw your protagonist's plans into disarray, specifically highlighting their flaws in the process.
2. Show the aftermath of your protagonist's failure and make them question their journey thus far.
3. Give your protagonist a glimmer of hope and help them finally overcome their inner struggle.
4. Guide your cast as they regroup and march forward towards the Climax.

Day Nine: The Final Fight

1. Visualize your Climax, taking notes on any important elements.
2. Finalize any of your cast's preparations before triggering the final confrontation of your story.
3. Begin your story's Climax, paying special attention to how your protagonist will resolve the conflict.
4. Decide on your protagonist's final outcome—positive, flat, or negative—and use that to write the final moments of your Climax.

Day Ten: Dawn of the Last Day

1. Decide how to spend your story's final moments.

2. Show the consequences of your story's Climax and hint at how your cast's lives might go on from here.
3. Say one last goodbye to your story's world and characters.
4. Celebrate! You've earned it.

GLOSSARY

Below you'll find a short glossary of the most important writing terms mentioned throughout this challenge. Each one will include its definition, as well as where it first appeared in this book.

———

Character Arc - Day Two:

The inner emotional journey a character goes on throughout your story. There are three primary character arcs in total: positive arcs, negative arcs, and flat arcs.

Core Conflict - Day Two:

The primary conflict of your story, this is the catalyst for both your plot, as well as your protagonist's character development. Most of your secondary conflicts and subplots will also tie into this core conflict.

Inner Editor - Day Two:

The harsh inner voice most writers experience when writing their novels. This voice pushes us to be overly critical of our work, and has a habit of derailing our progress.

Outline - Day Zero:

A document that catalogs all the most important information about your story. Typically, this includes things like your plot, your character's arcs and personalities, and any key details about your worldbuilding. If you're looking for more guidance on how to create an outline of your own, check out The *Ten Day Outline*.

Point of View - Day One:

Typically abbreviated POV, this is the perspective from which your story is told. For instance, in First Person POV, your story is told by your protagonist using "I did, I thought, I felt, I saw, etc…"

Scenes - Day Four:

These are the building blocks of your novel, acting as the individual units your story is built from.

Scene Structure - Day Four:

Much like story structure, scene structure describes the common patterns found in well-written scenes. Most scenes follow a basic Action and Reaction structure.

Story Structure - Day Three:

Culturally recognized ways of telling stories based on common patterns, plot points, and conflicts. Perhaps the most famous example of this is The Three Act Structure.

Tense - Day One:

The grammatical form used to indicate when something is happening and when that action was completed. For example, walk is present tense, while walked is past tense. Typically, your story should be told in a single tense.

The Three Act Structure - Day Three:

One of the most popular forms of story structure found in Western storytelling, this structure is based on a set of three acts: Act 1 (the setup), Act 2 (the confrontation), and Act 3 (the resolution).

Writer's Voice - Day One:

The distinct style of prose a writer uses when telling their stories. Typically, this voice is defined by their word choice and tone, as well as the unique perspective they show through their writing.

"Close the door. Write with no one looking over your shoulder. Don't try to figure out what other people want to hear from you; figure out what you have to say. It's the one and only thing you have to offer."

BARBARA KINGSOLVER, AMERICAN NOVELIST AND
POET

ALSO BY LEWIS JORSTAD

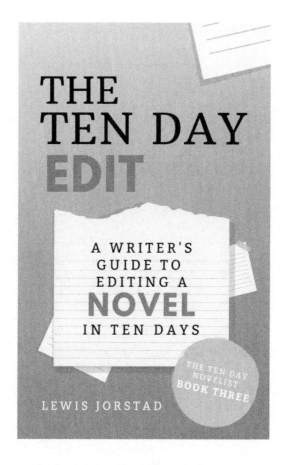

You've written a novel—now to perfect it.

If you're ready to go from first draft to finished novel, check out the next book in The Ten Day Novelist series: The Ten Day Edit!

Printed in Great Britain
by Amazon